My name is

_____

Phone number

_____

E.Mail

_____

CALLIGRAPHY
AND
HAND WRITING BOOK

"No part of this publication may be reproduced, distributed, or transmitted in any form or by any means, including photocopying, recording, or other electronic or mechanical methods, or by any information storage and mrieval system without the prior written permission of the publisher, except in the case of very brief quotations embodied in critical reviews and certain other noncommercial uses permitted by copyright law."

A

𝒜

a

𝒶

B

$\mathscr{B}$

b

$\mathscr{b}$

C

𝒞

C

𝑐

D

𝒟

d

d

E

E

e

e

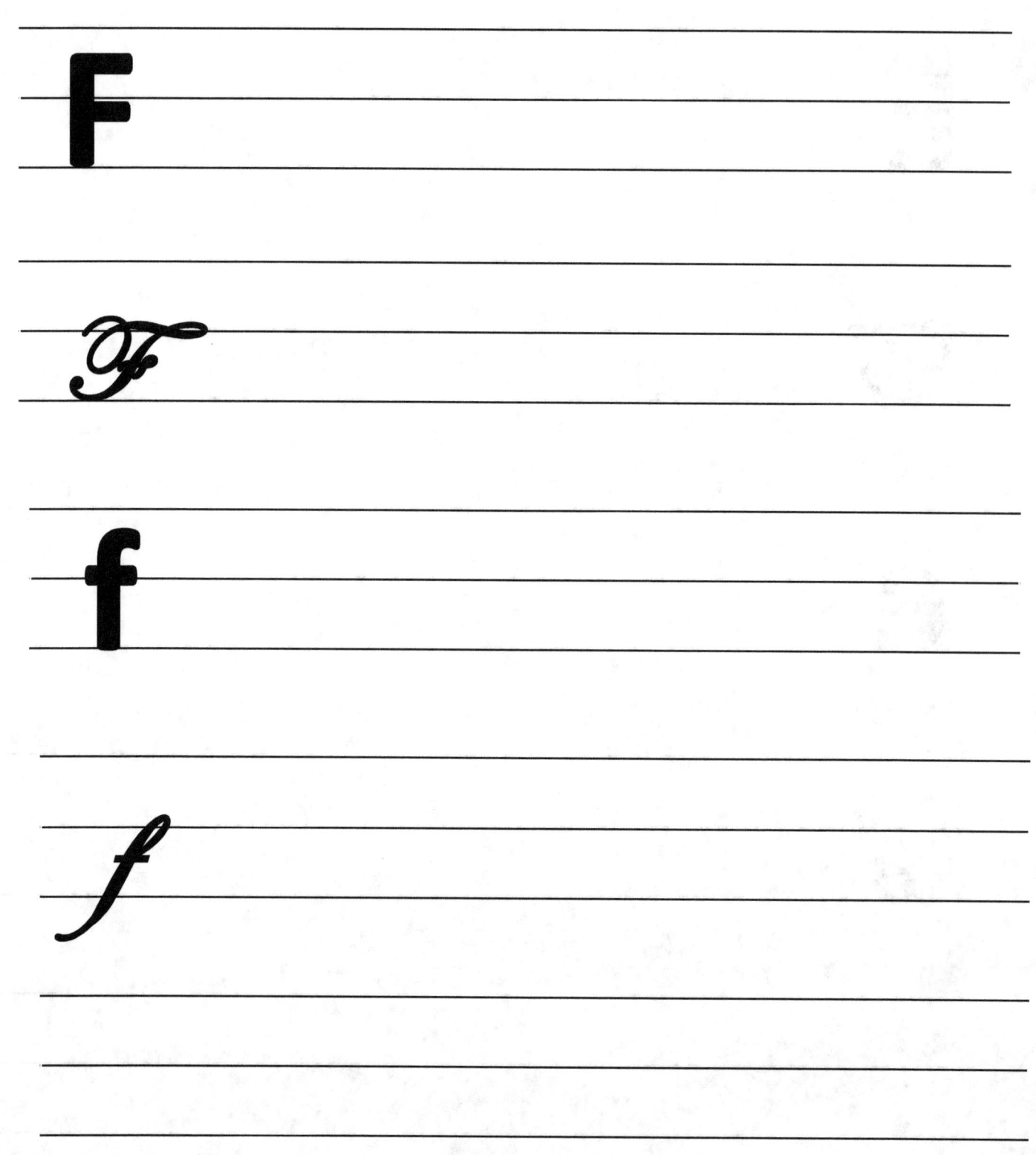

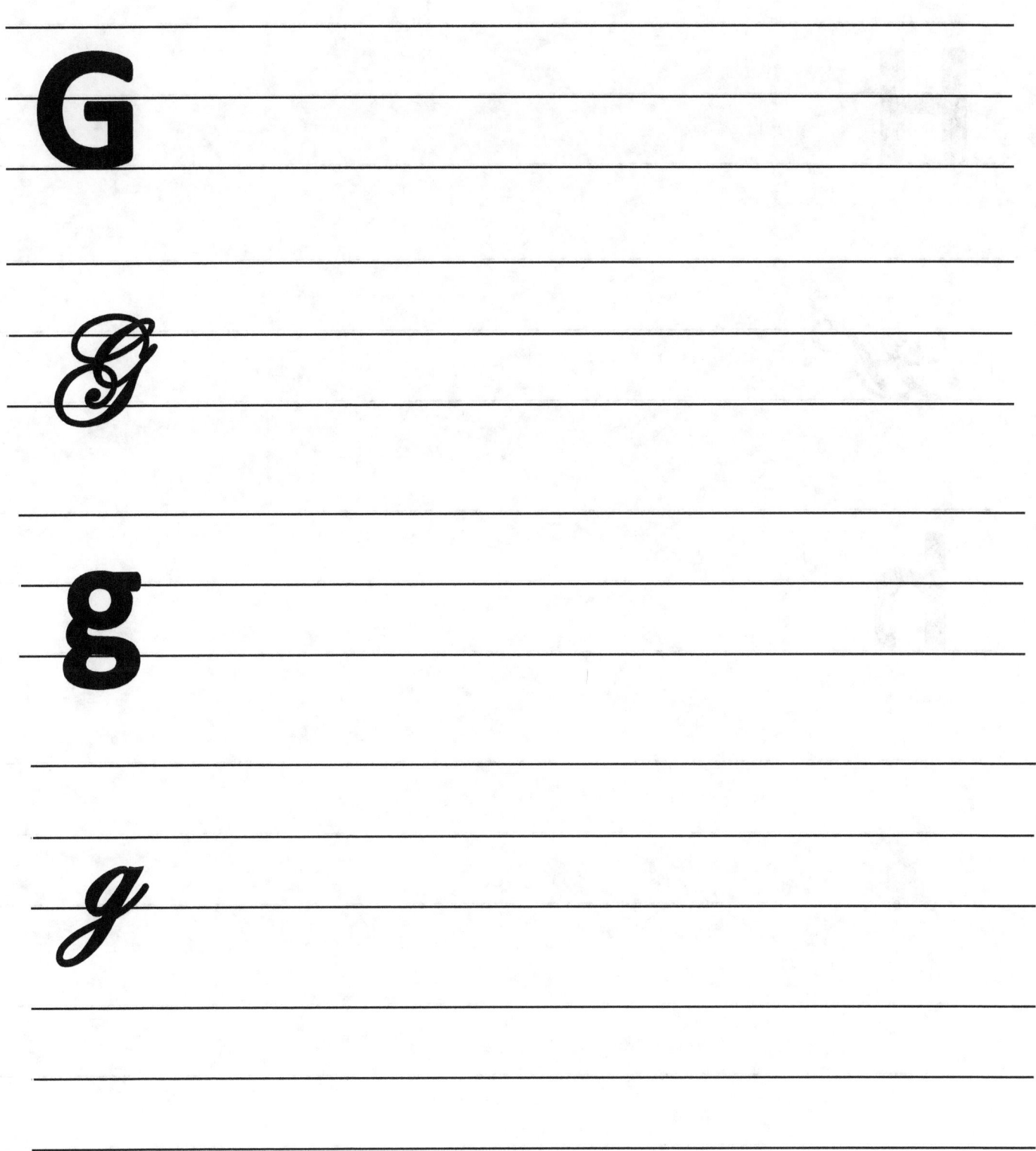

H

H

h

h

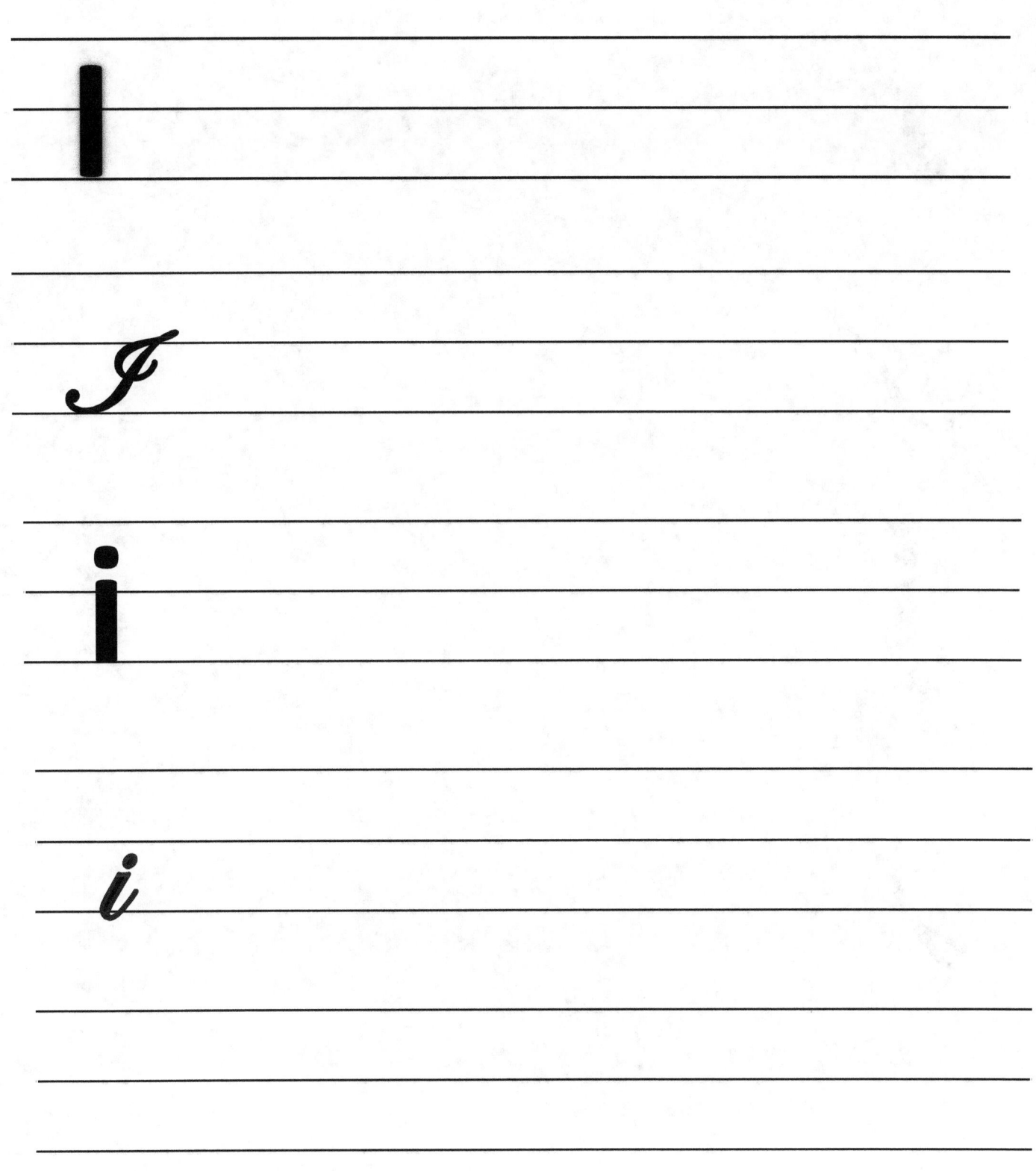

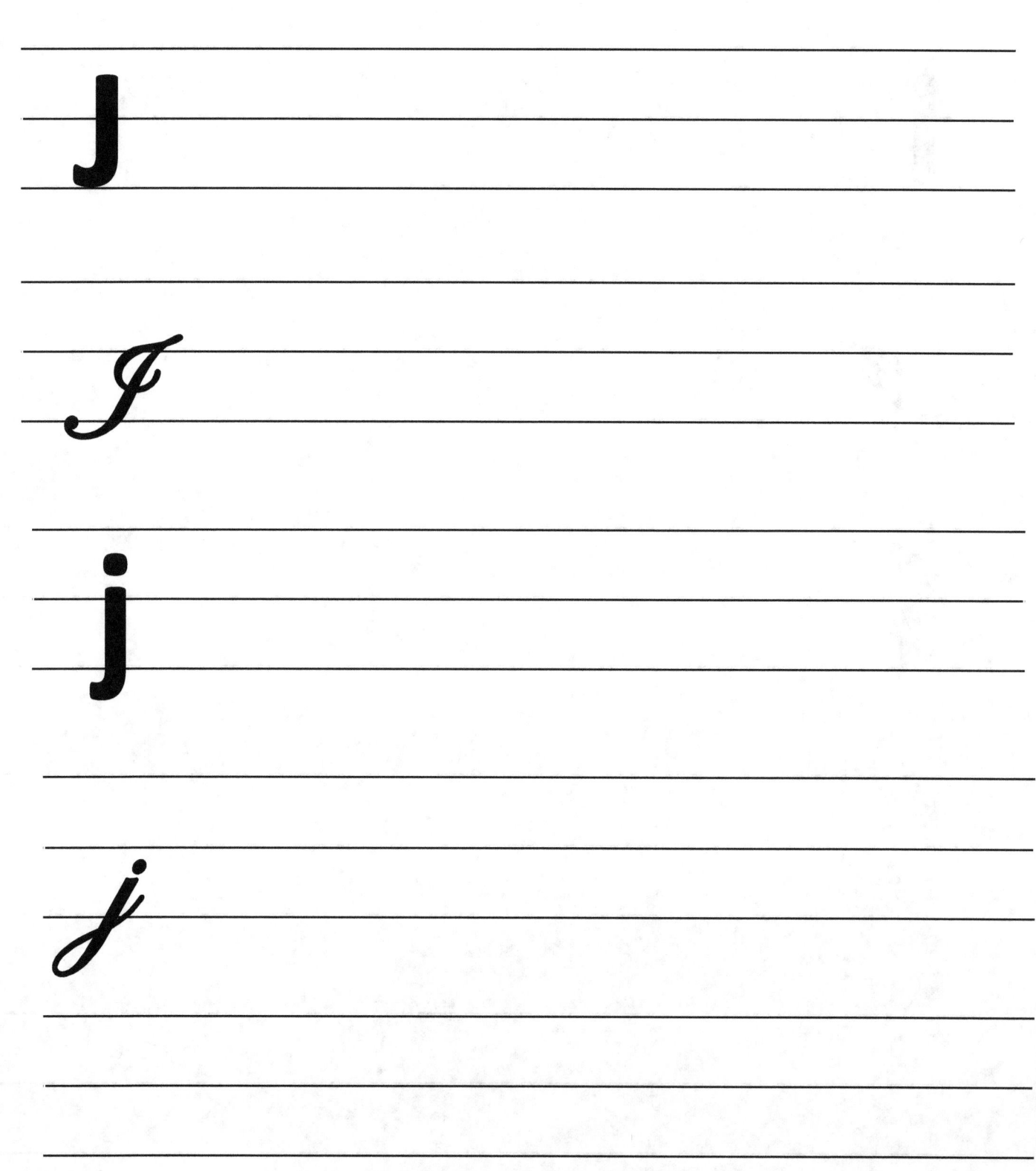

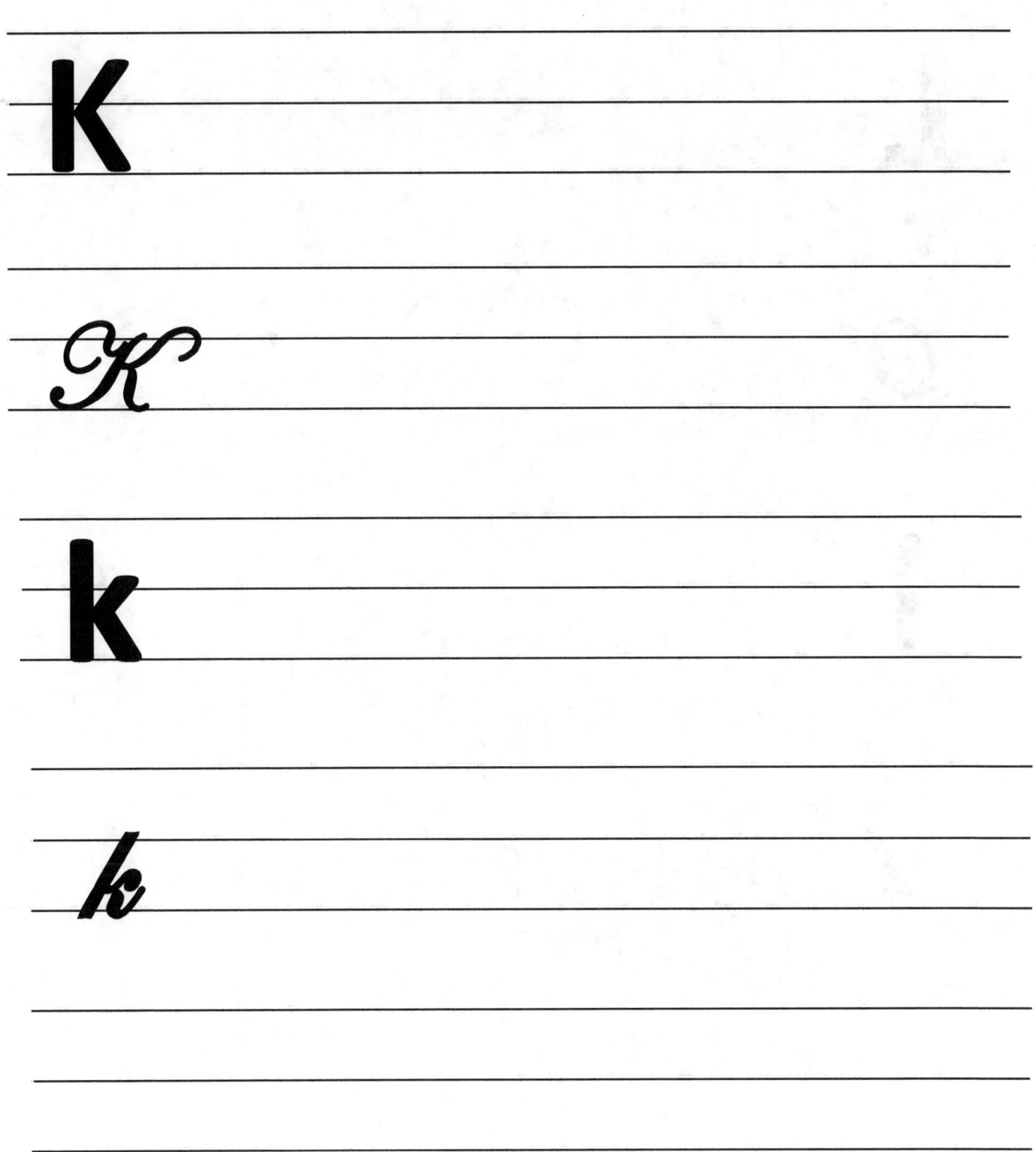

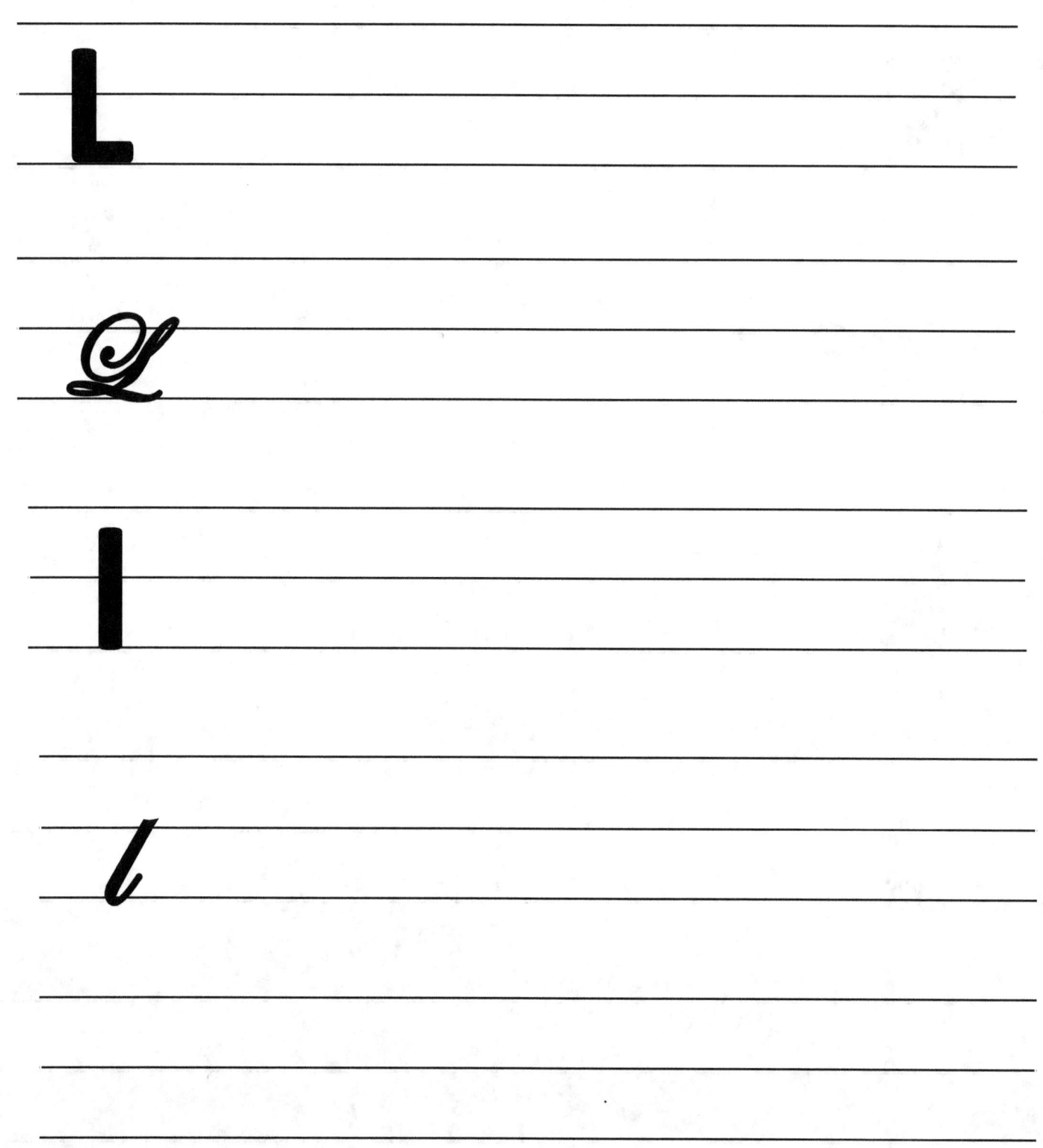

M

M

m

m

N

𝒩

n

𝓃

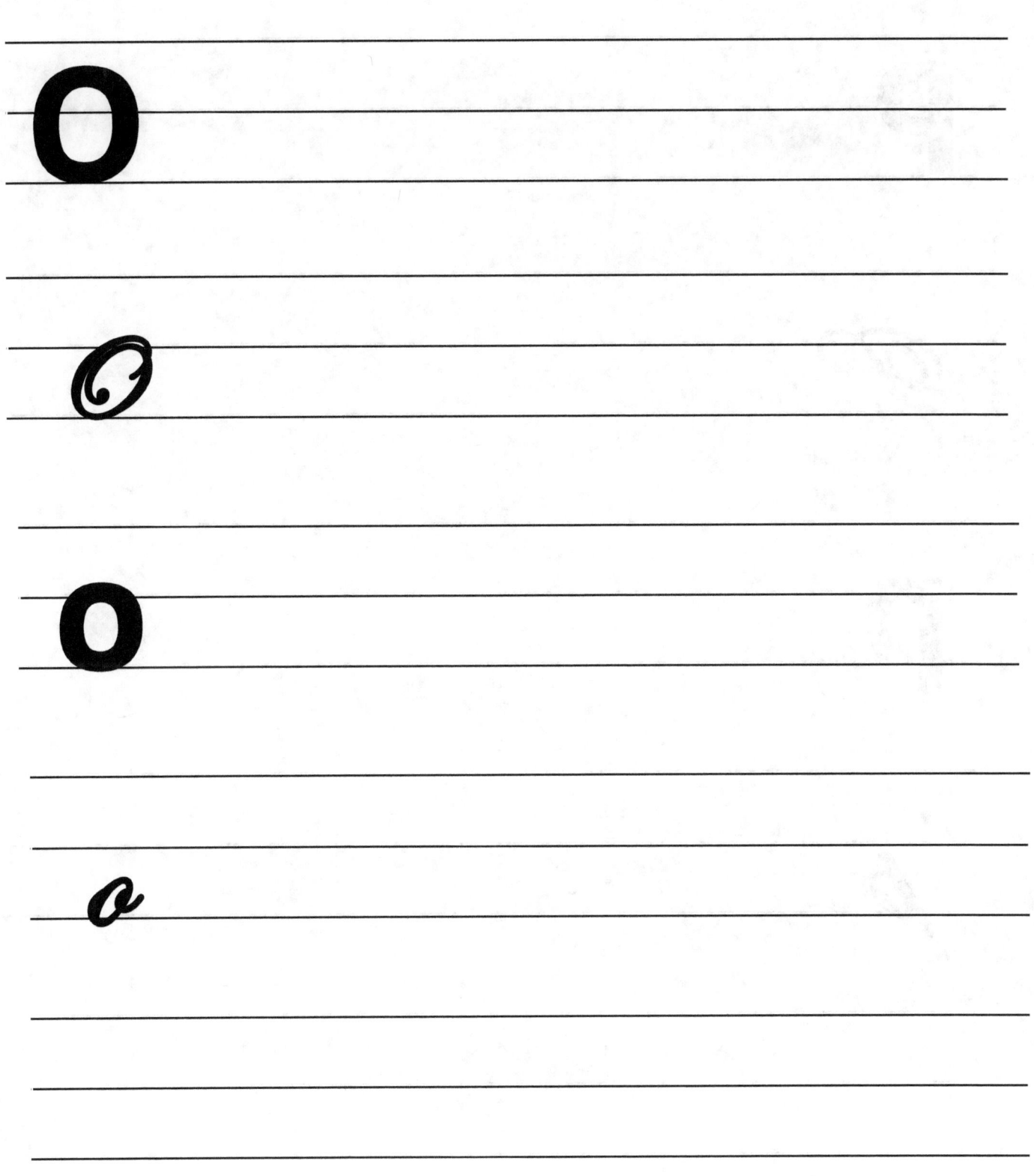

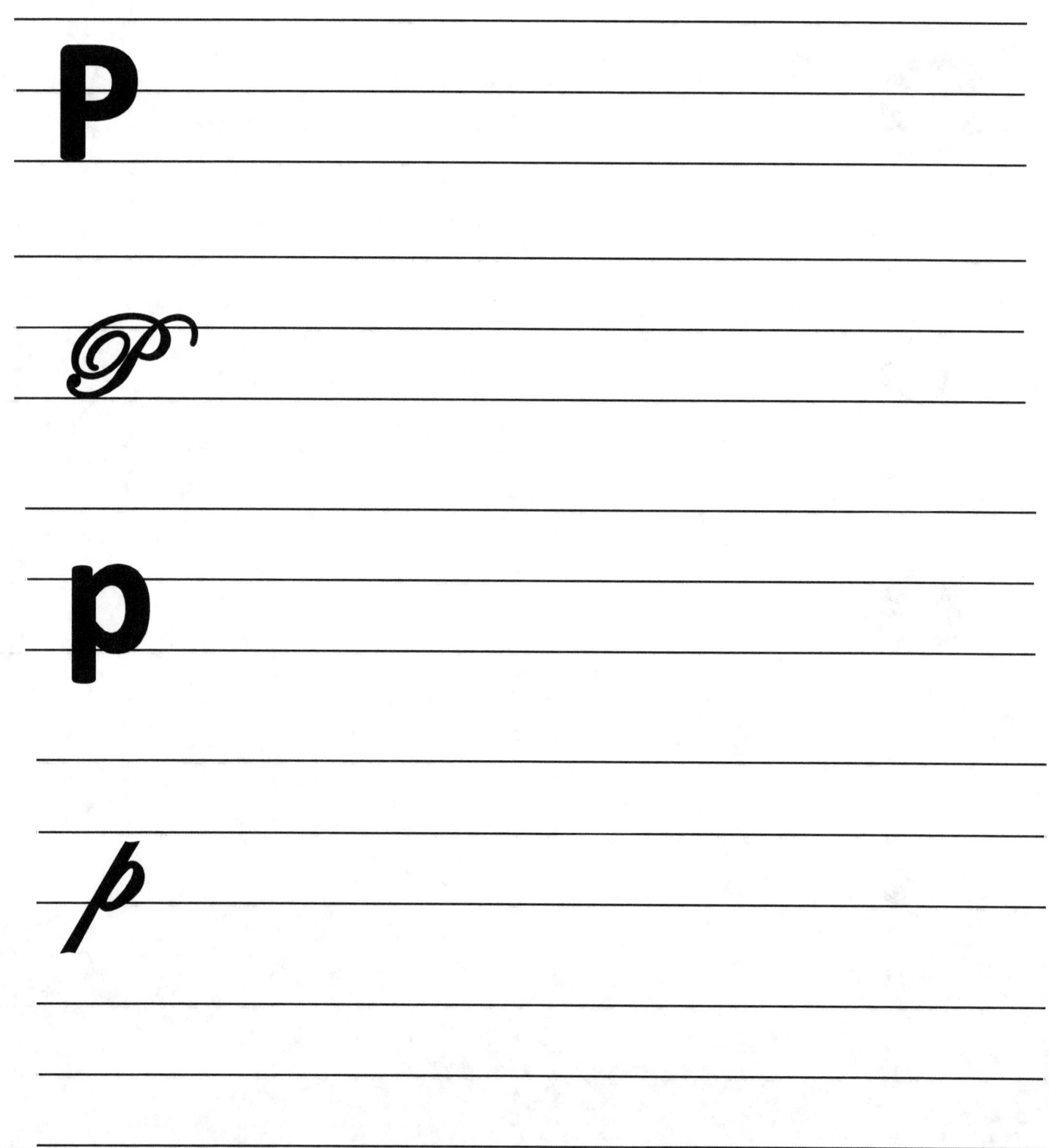

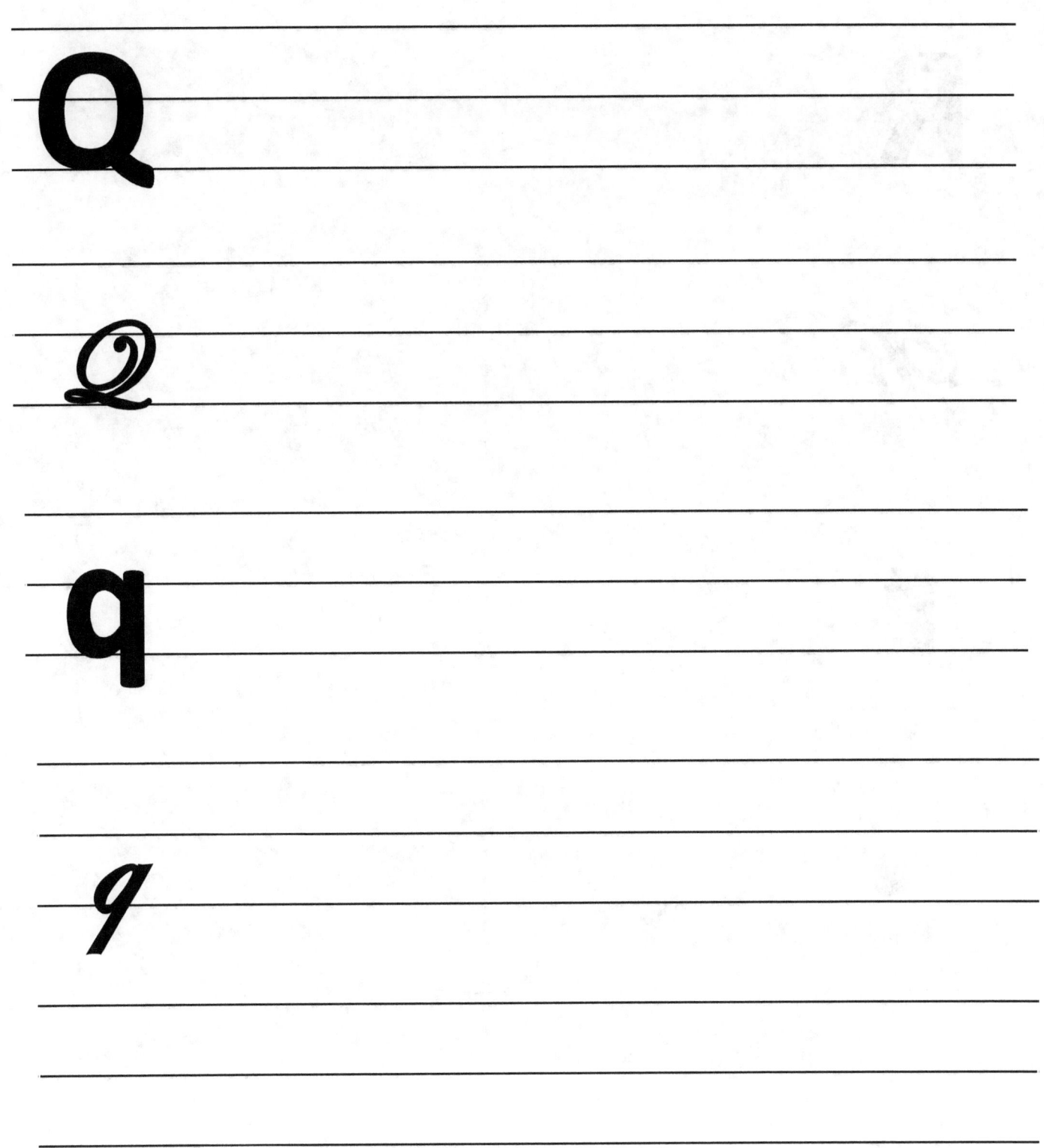

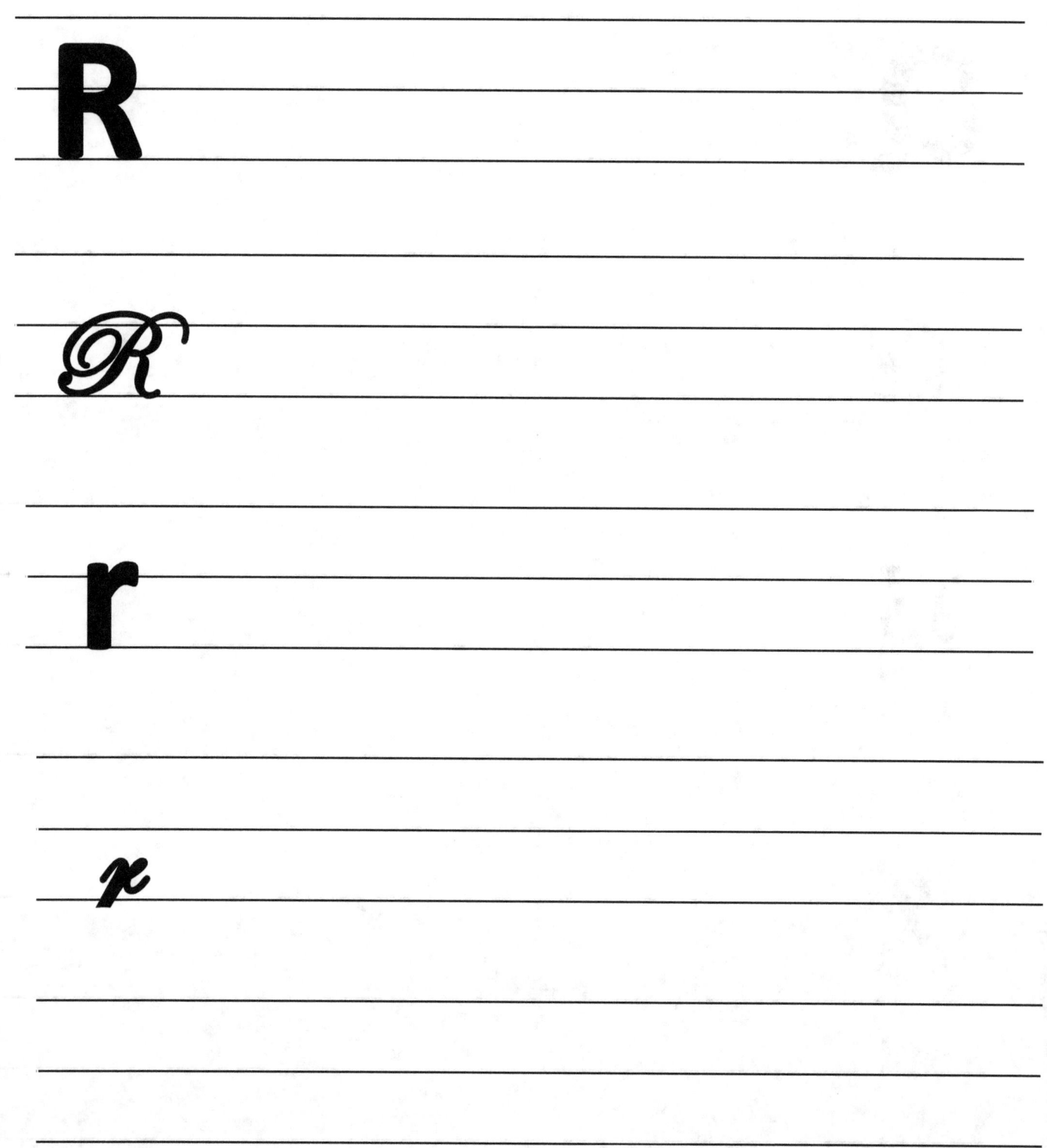

S

𝒮

S

𝓈

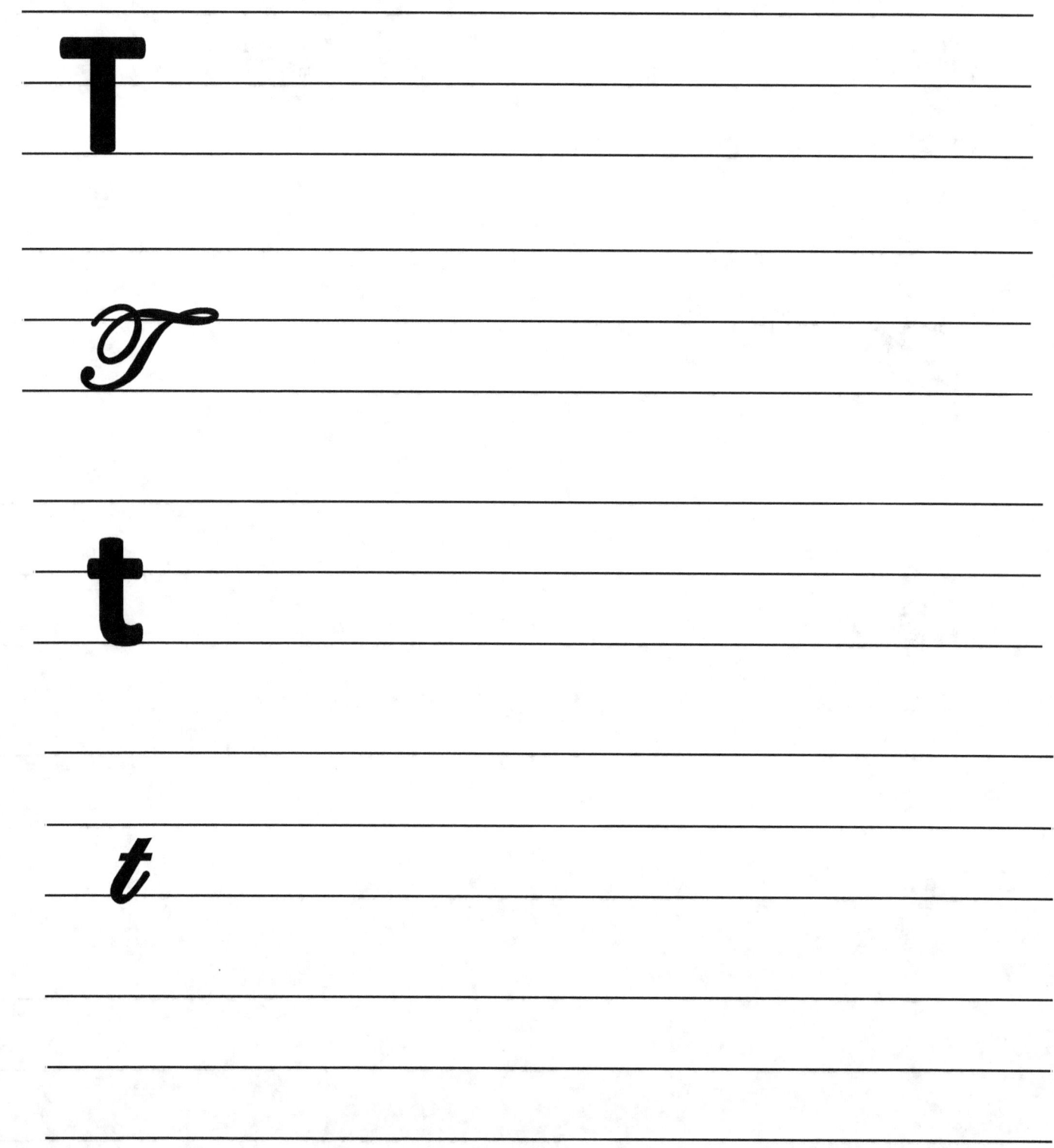

U

𝓤

u

𝓊

V

𝒱

v

𝓋

W

𝒲

W

𝓌

X

𝒳

X

𝓍

Y

𝒴

y

𝓎

Z

𝒵

z

𝓏

PRACTICING

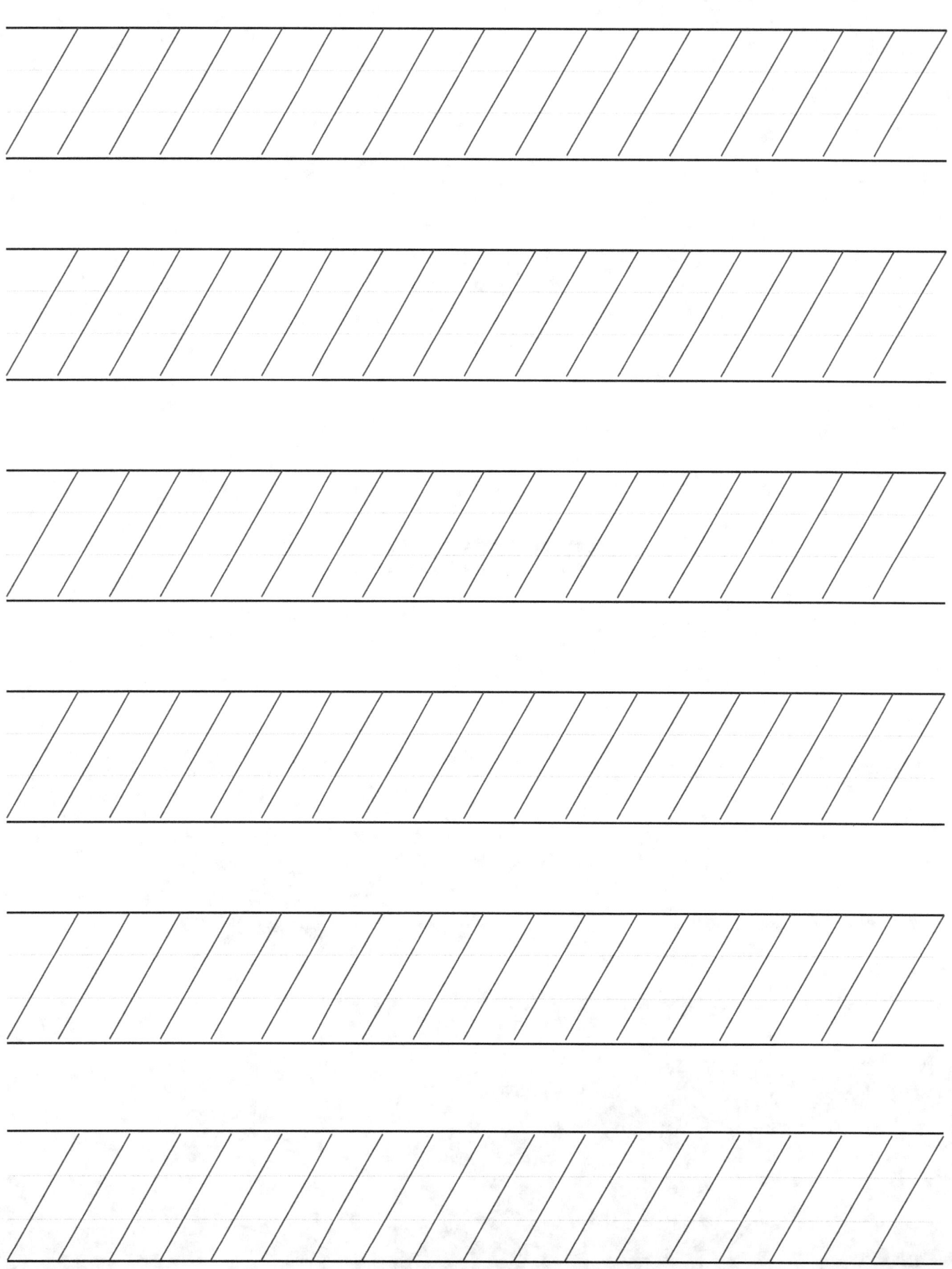

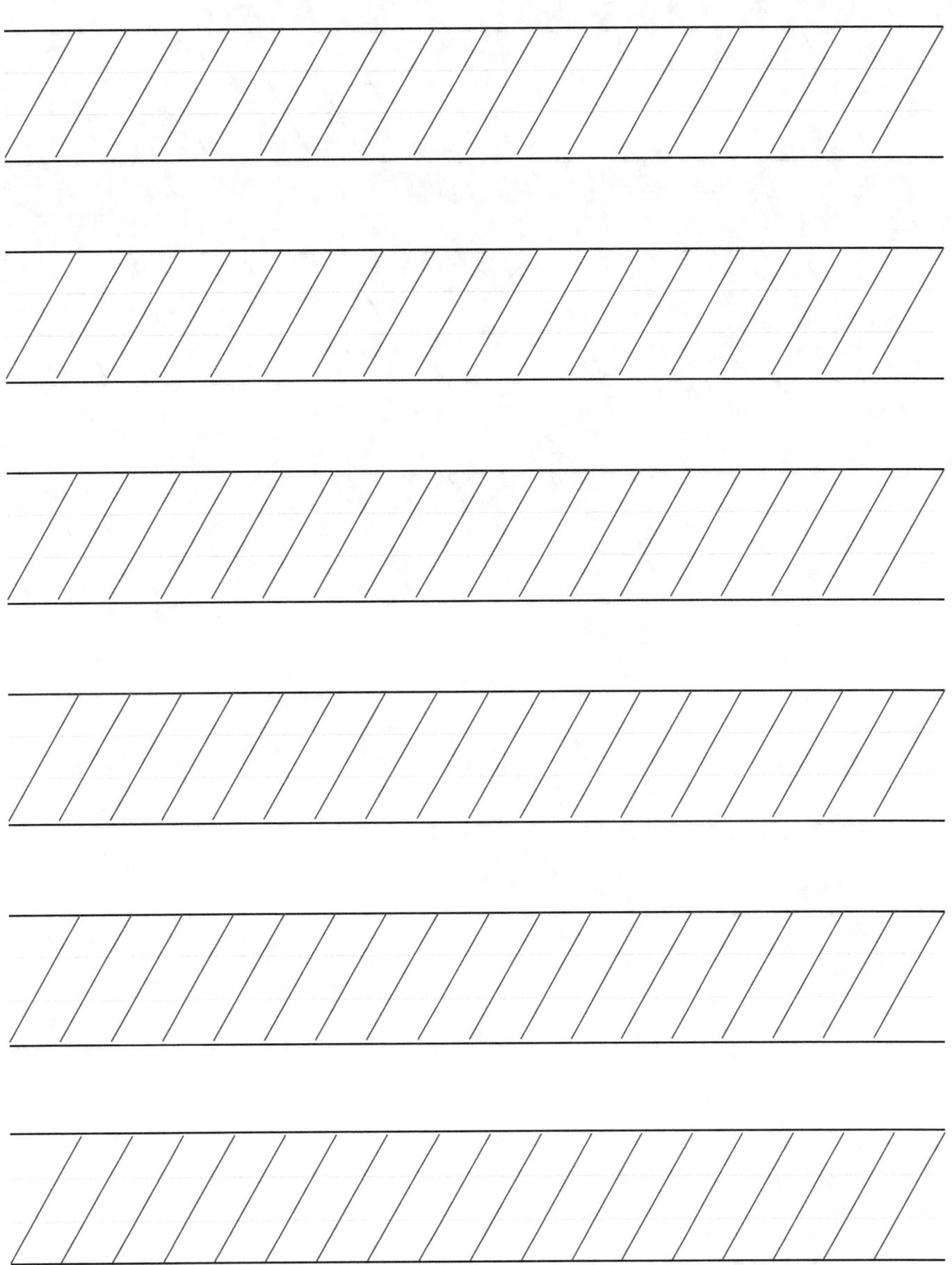

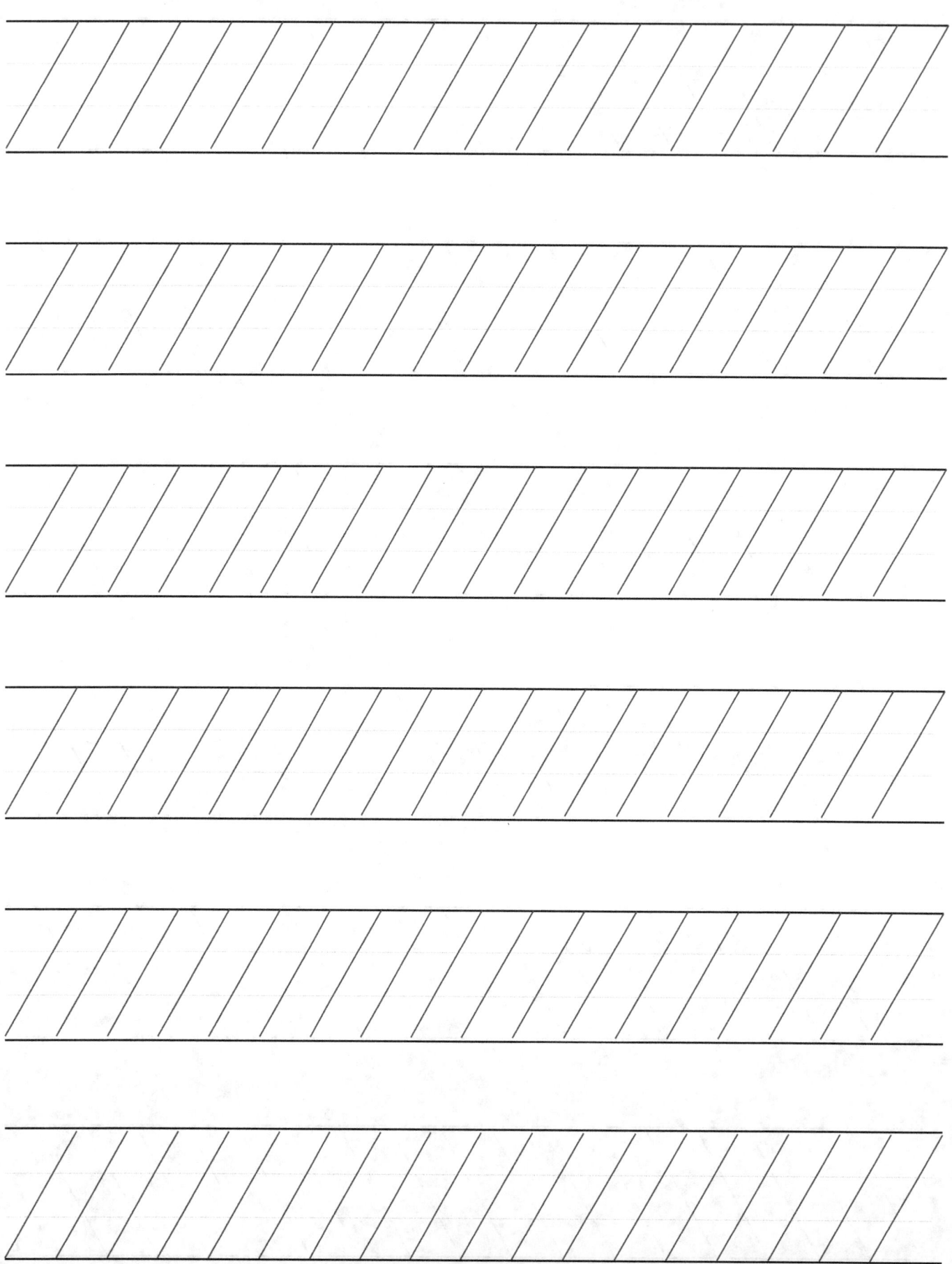

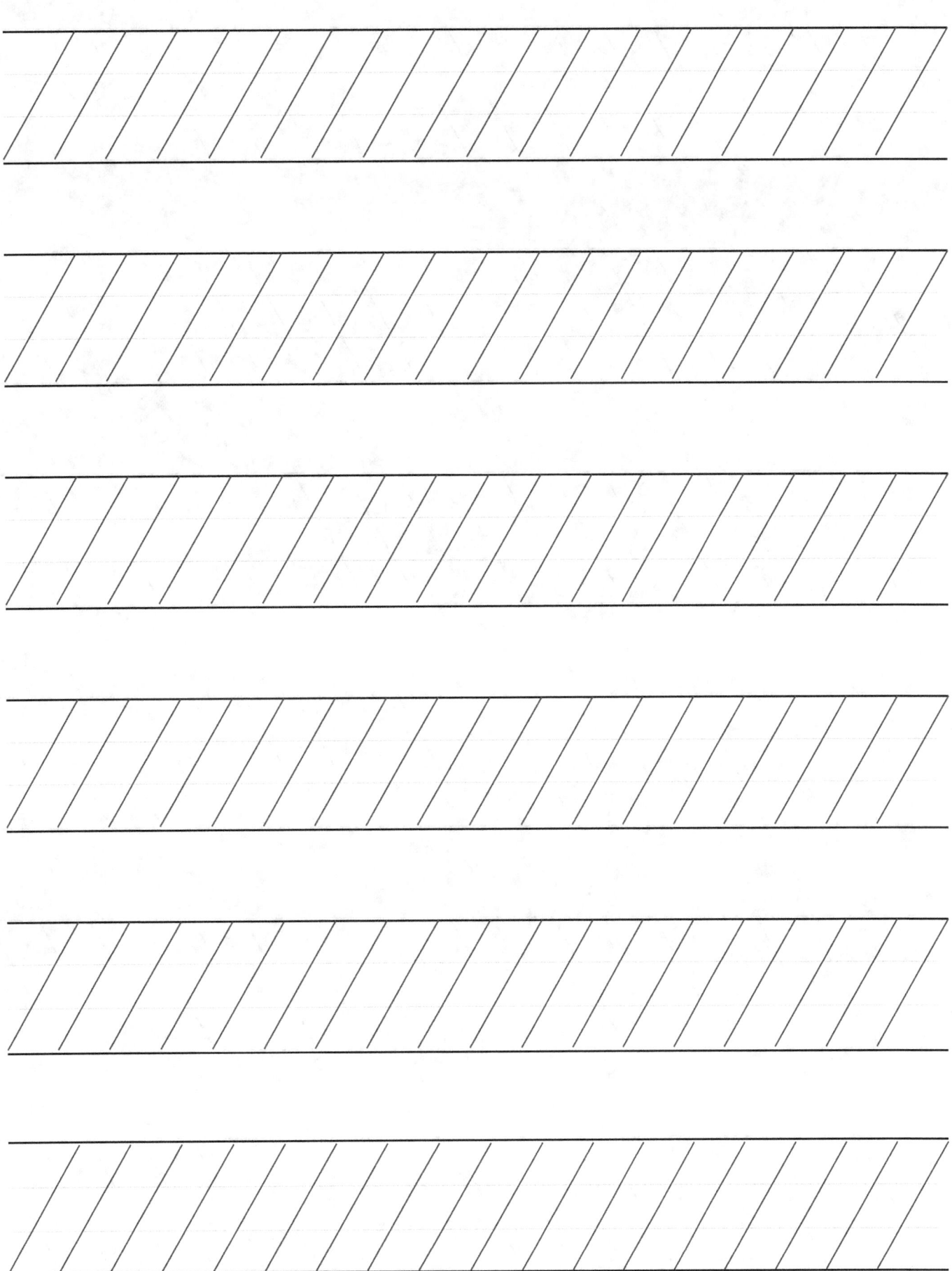

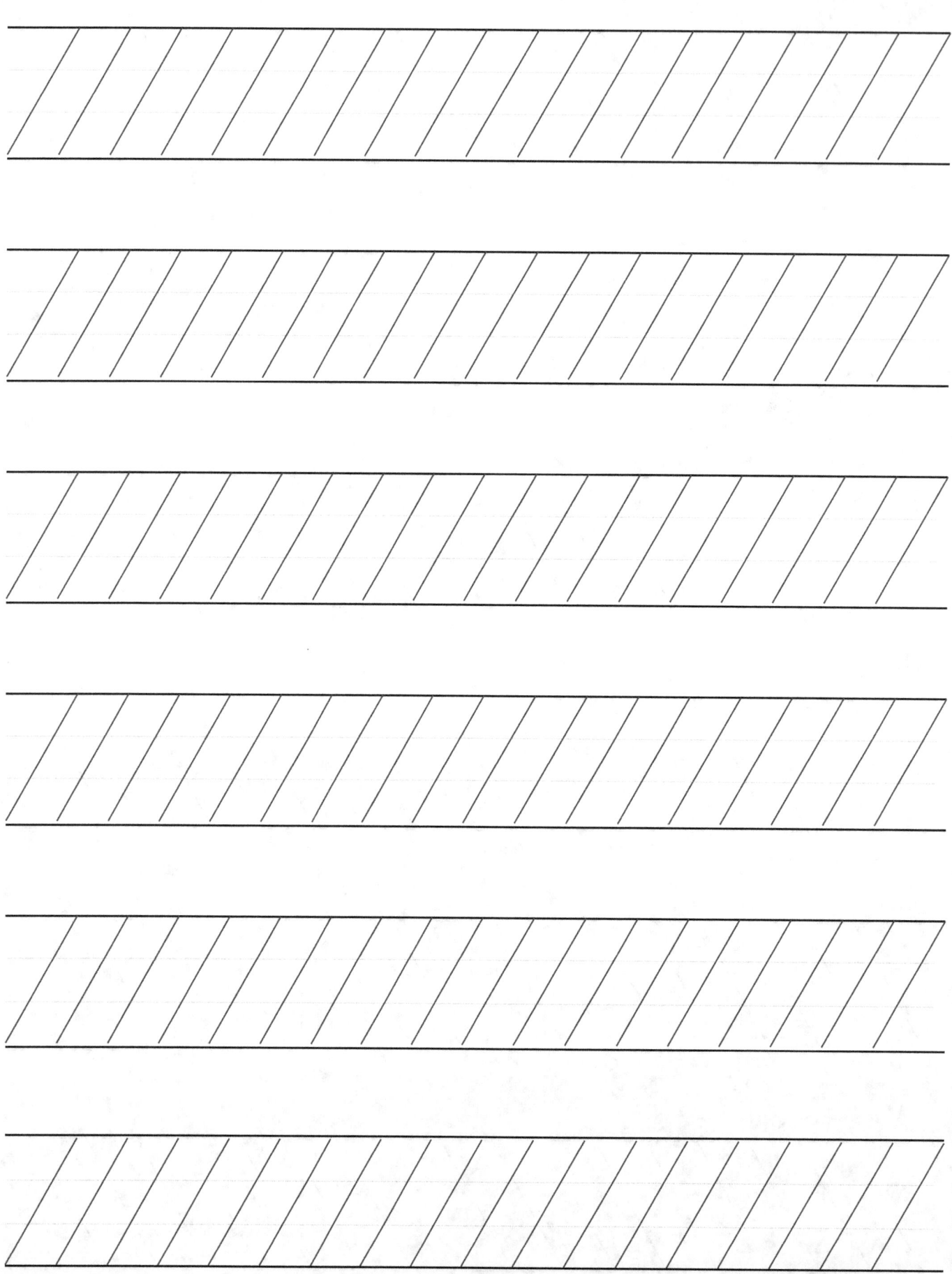

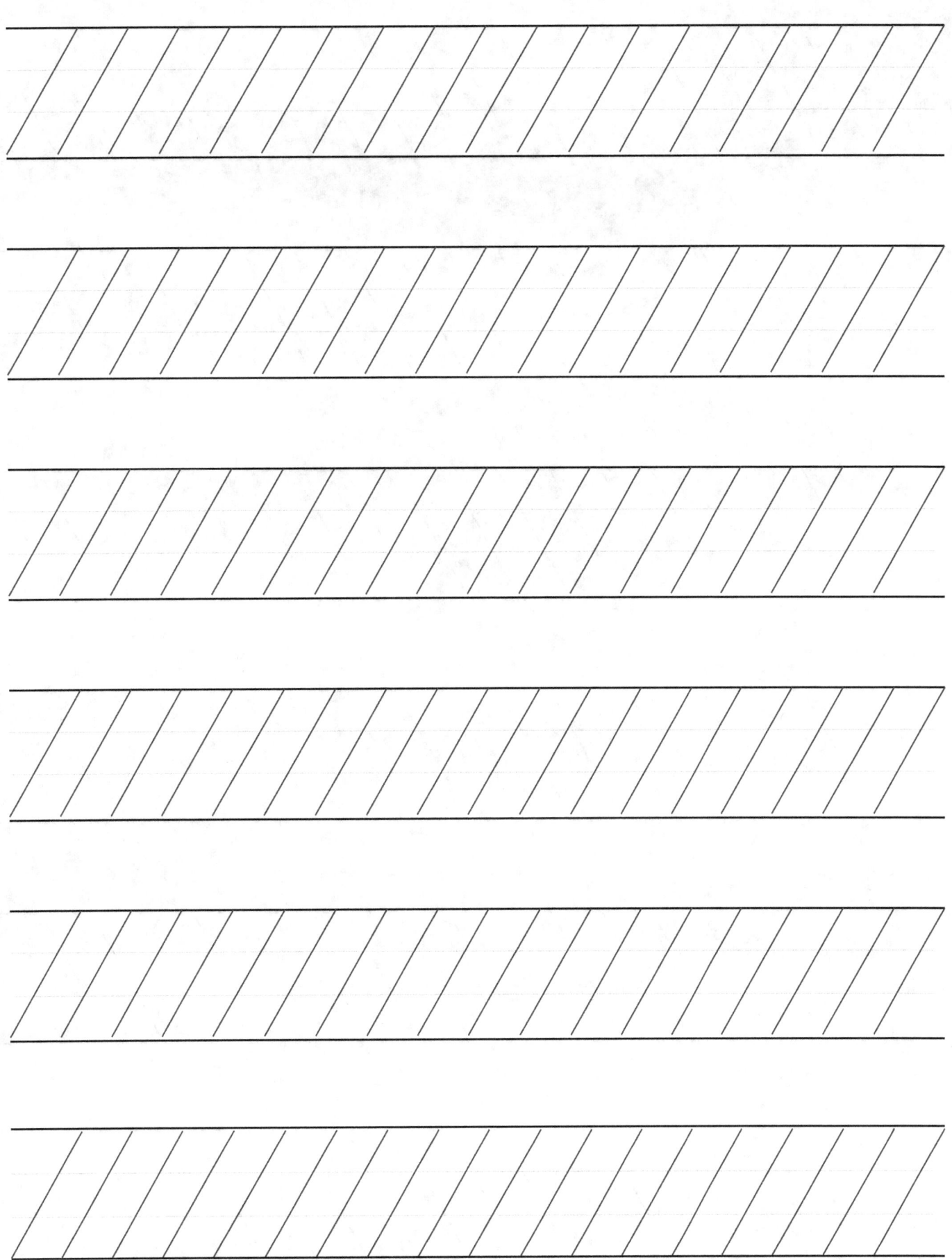

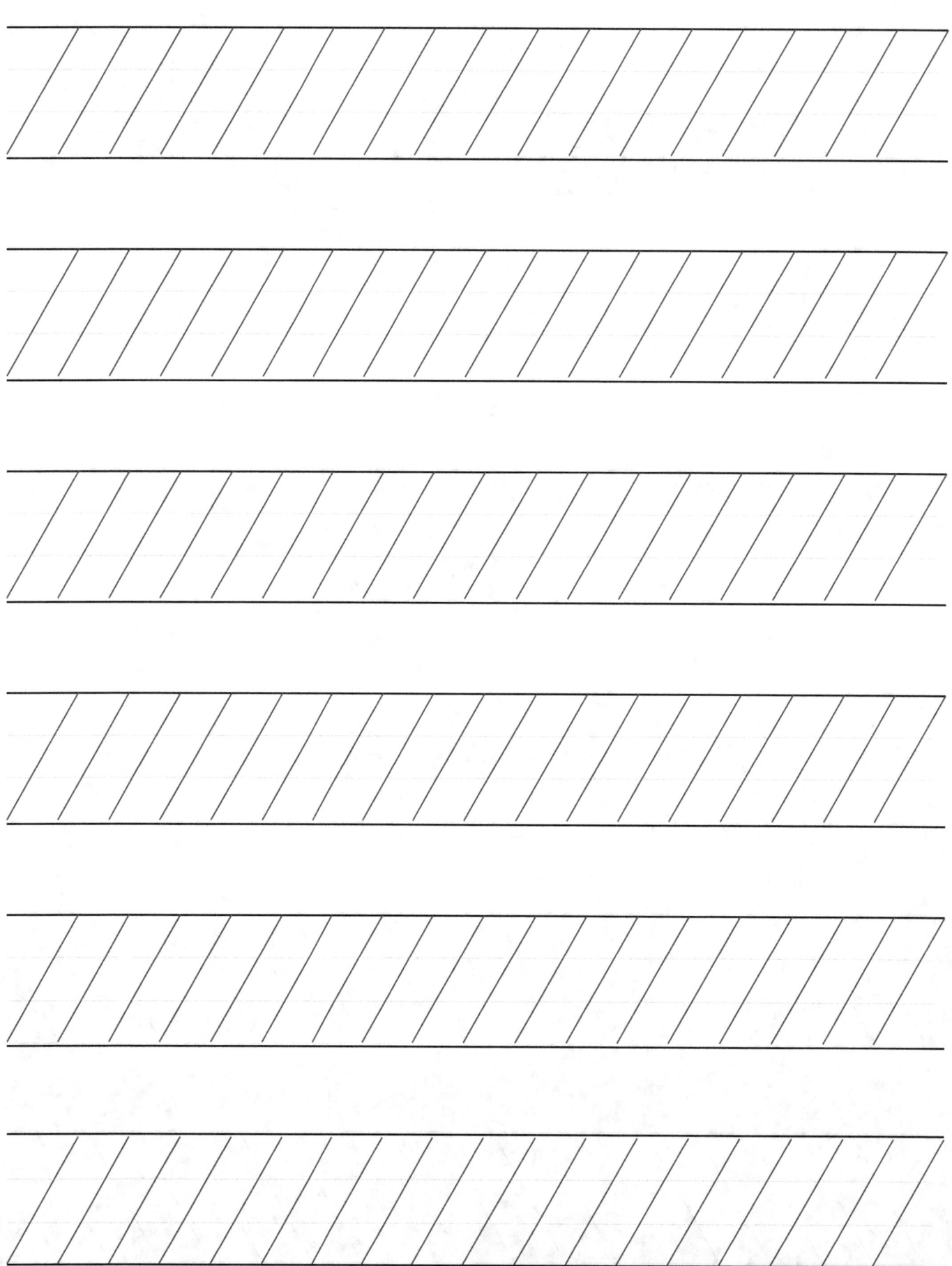

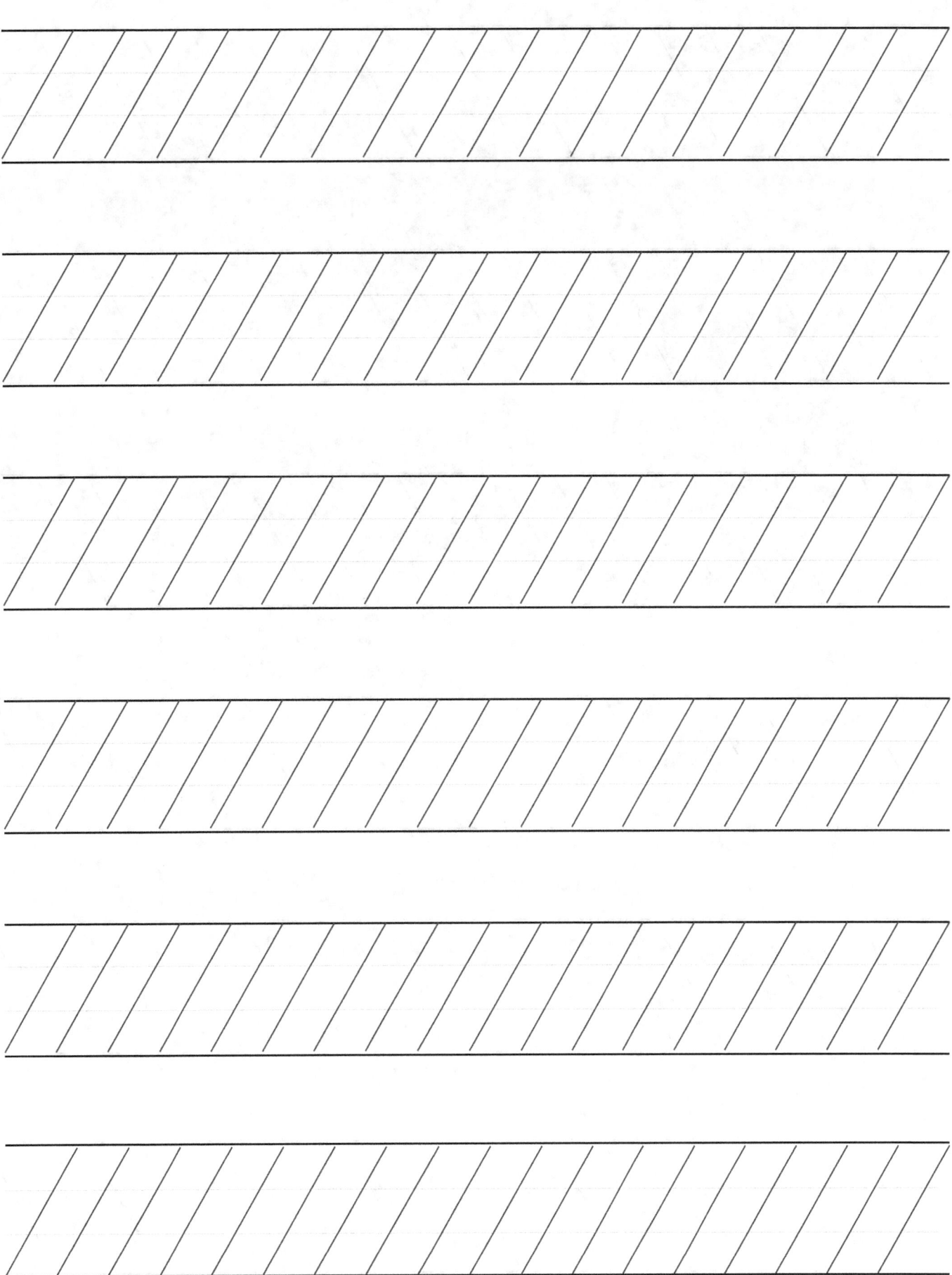

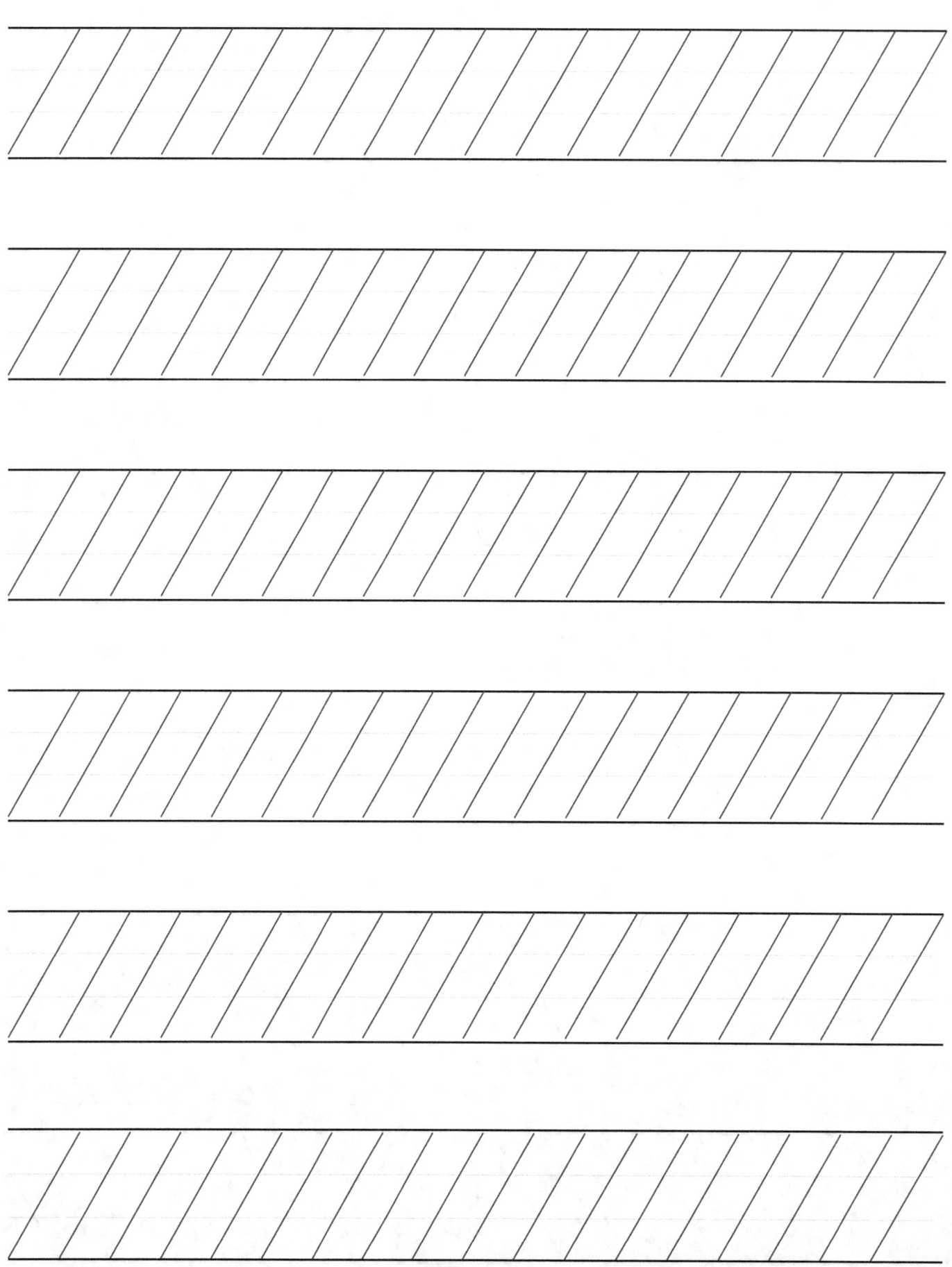

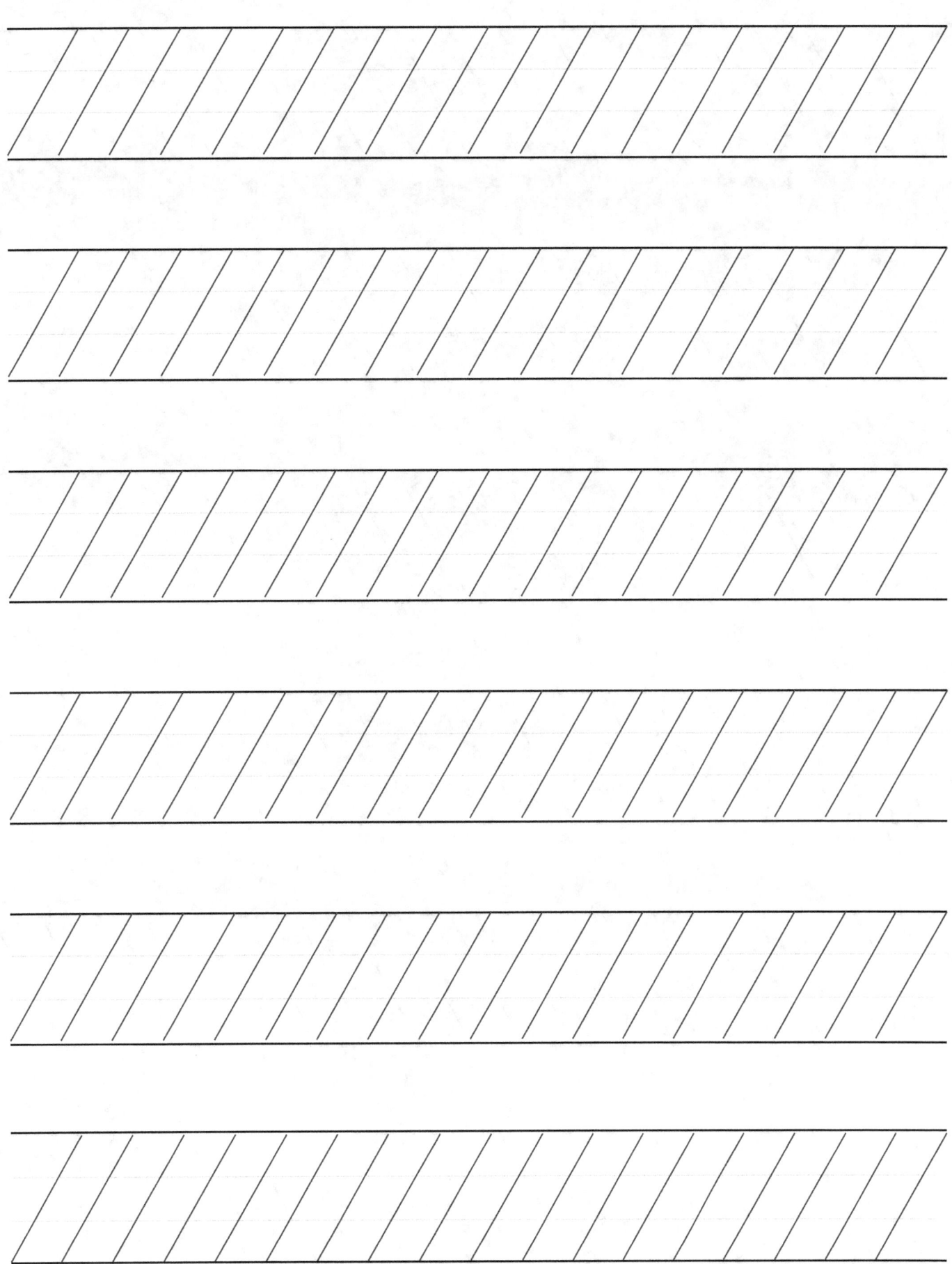

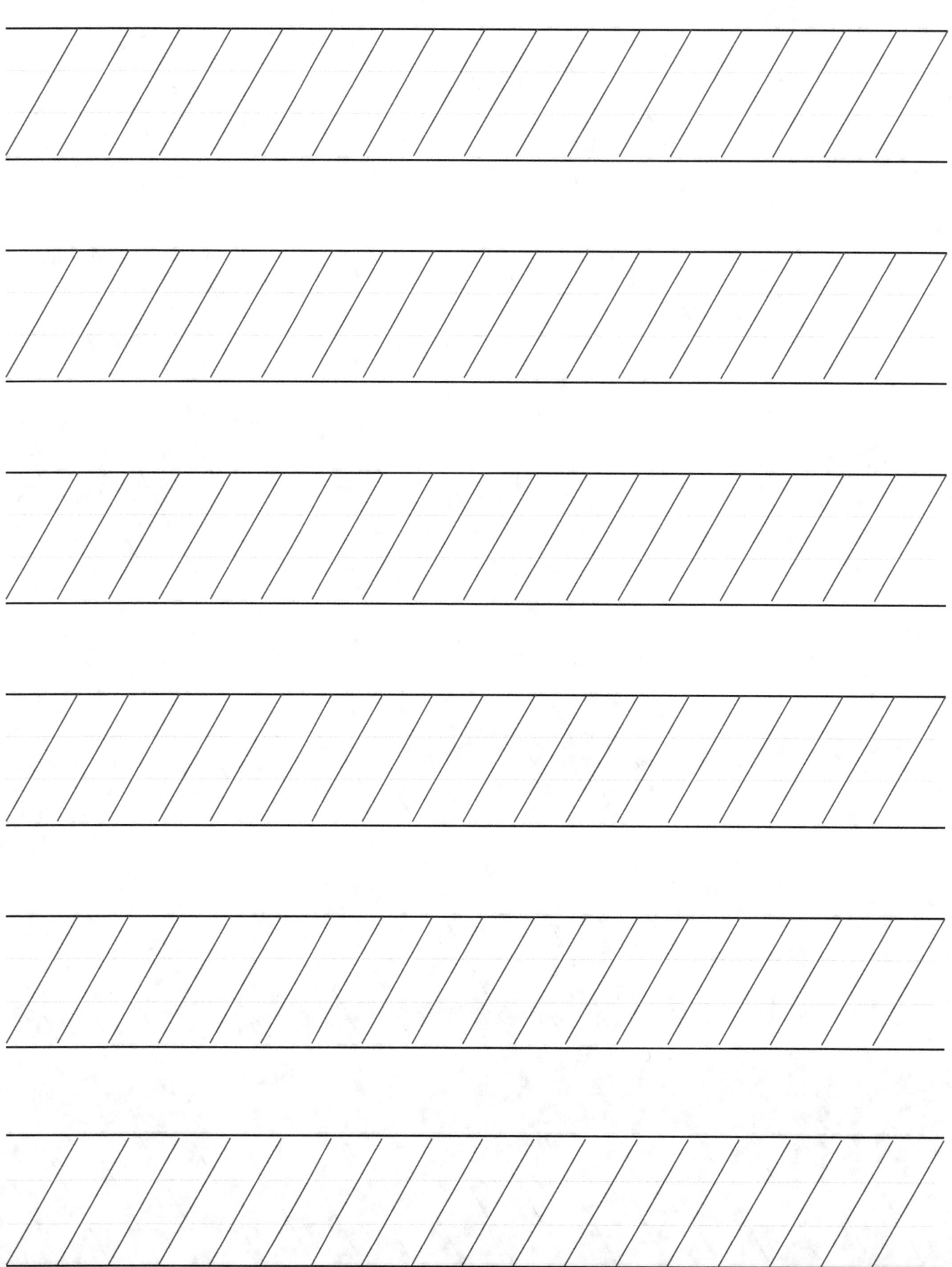

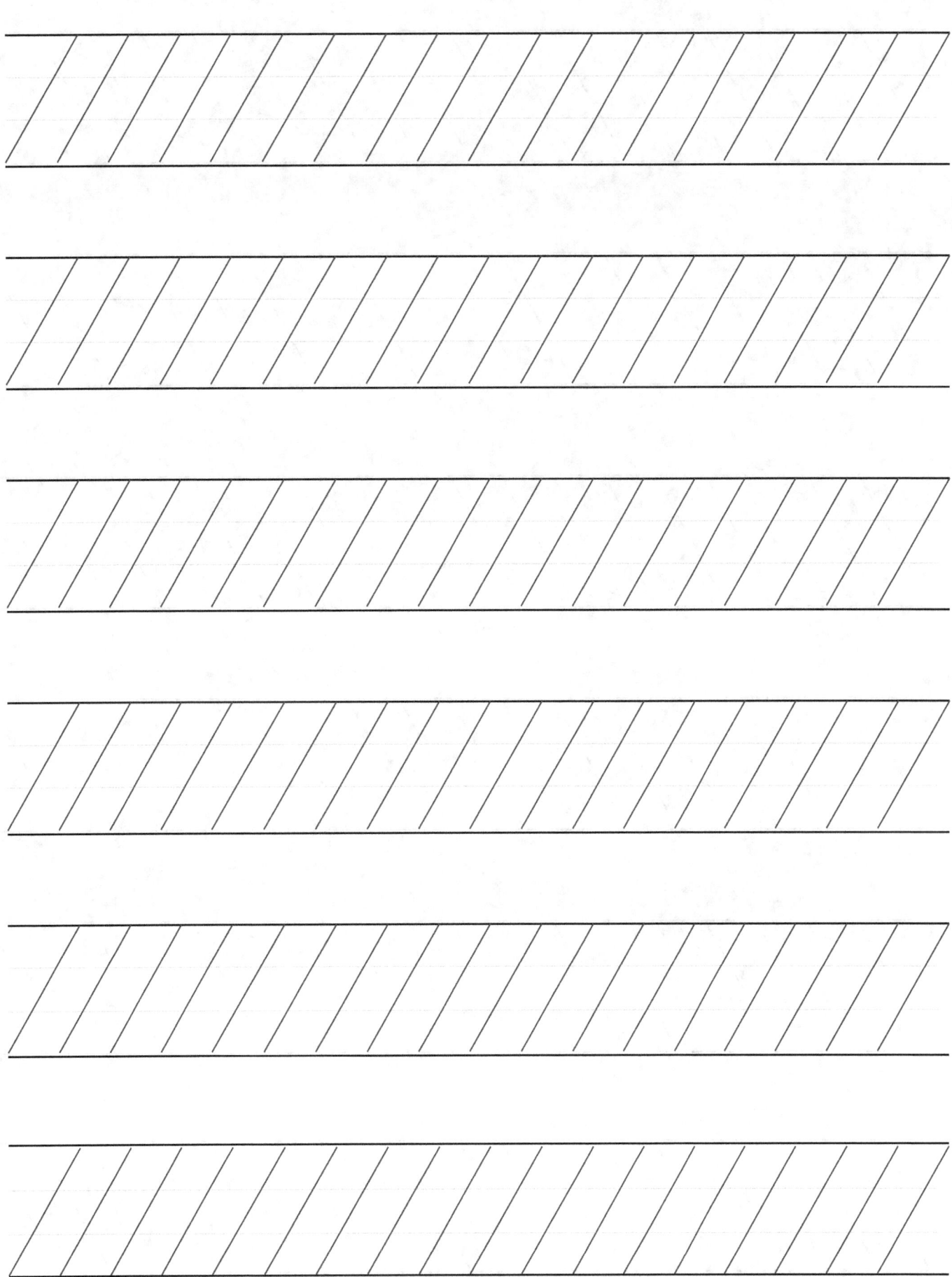

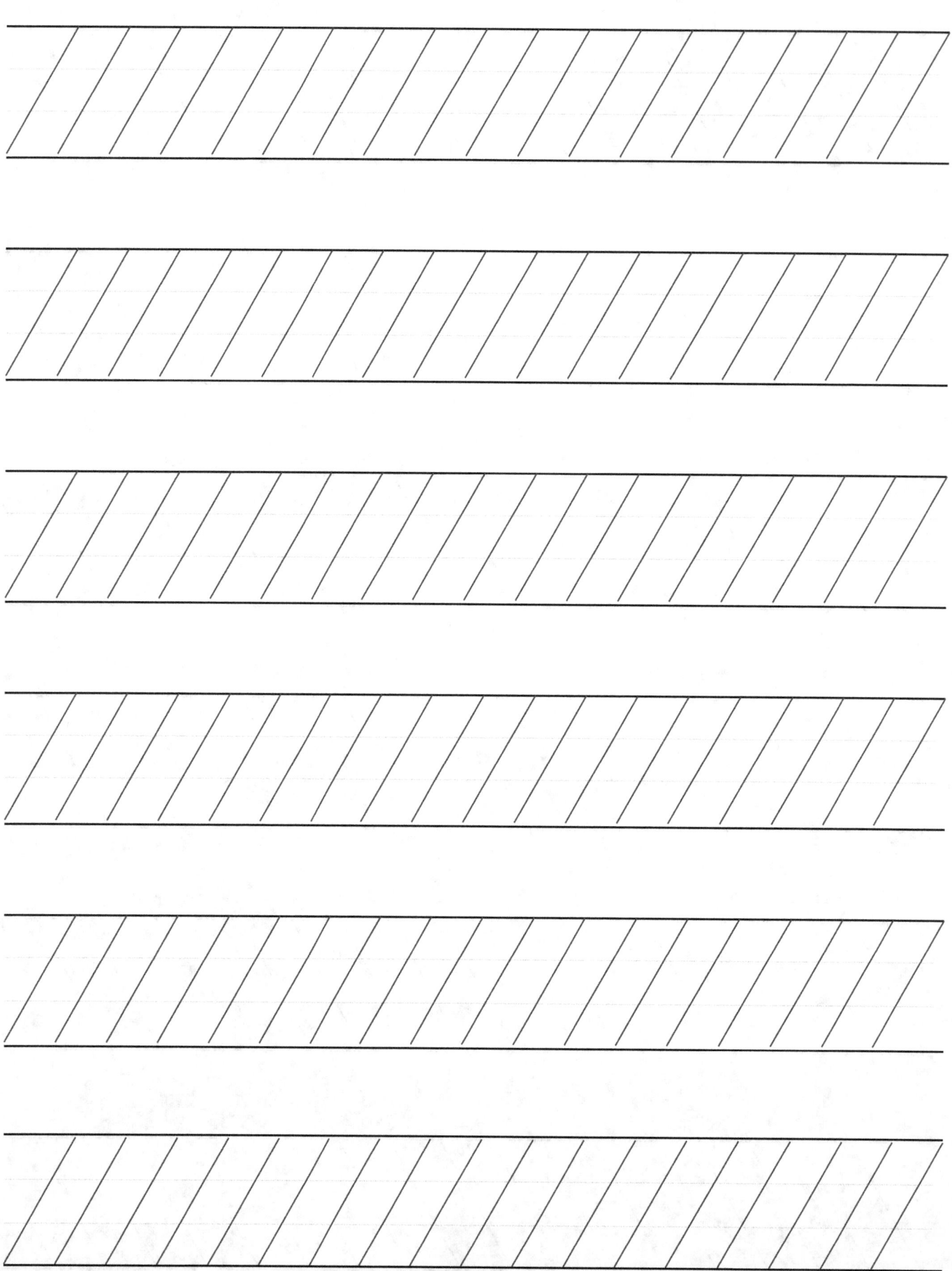

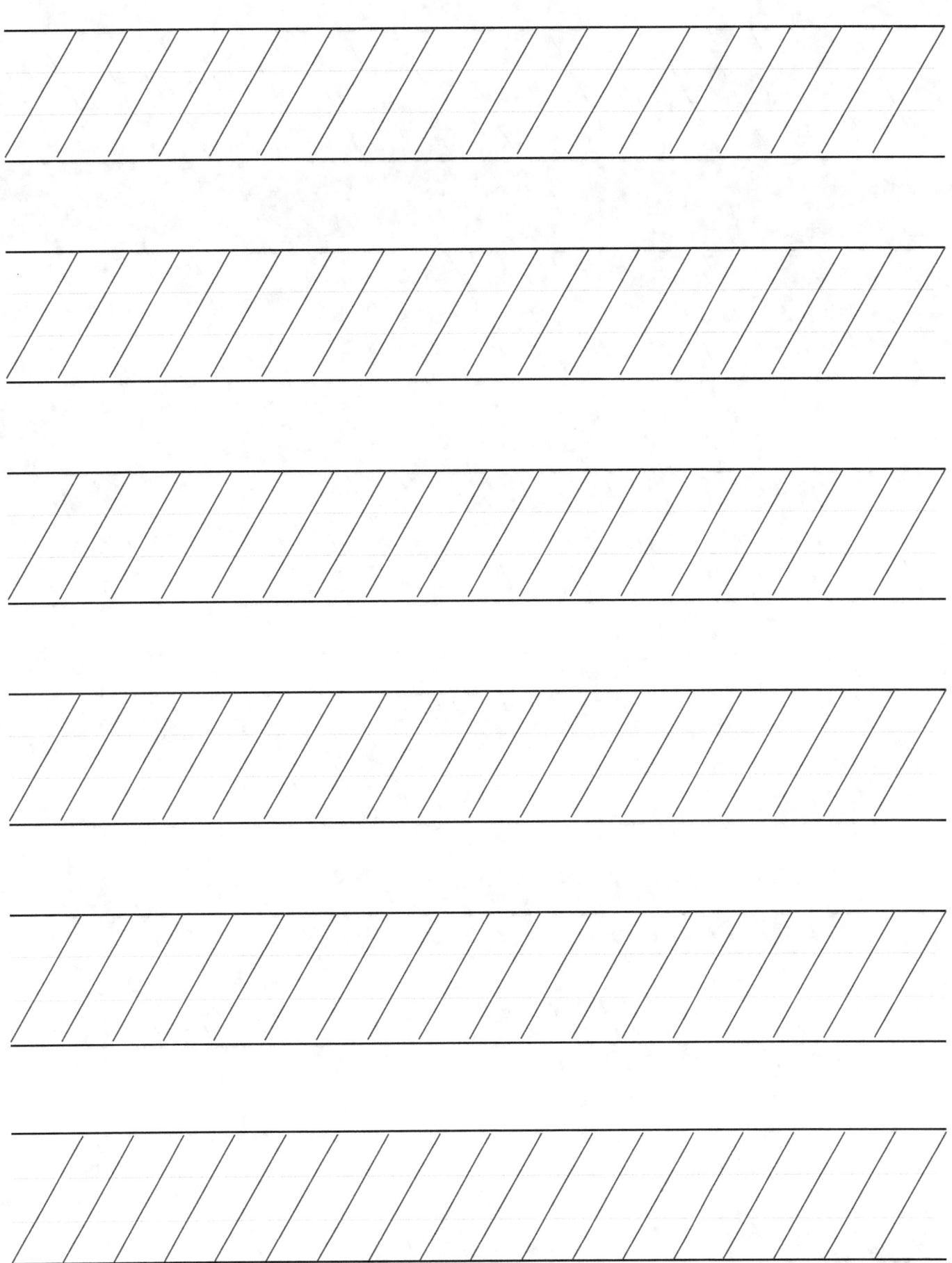

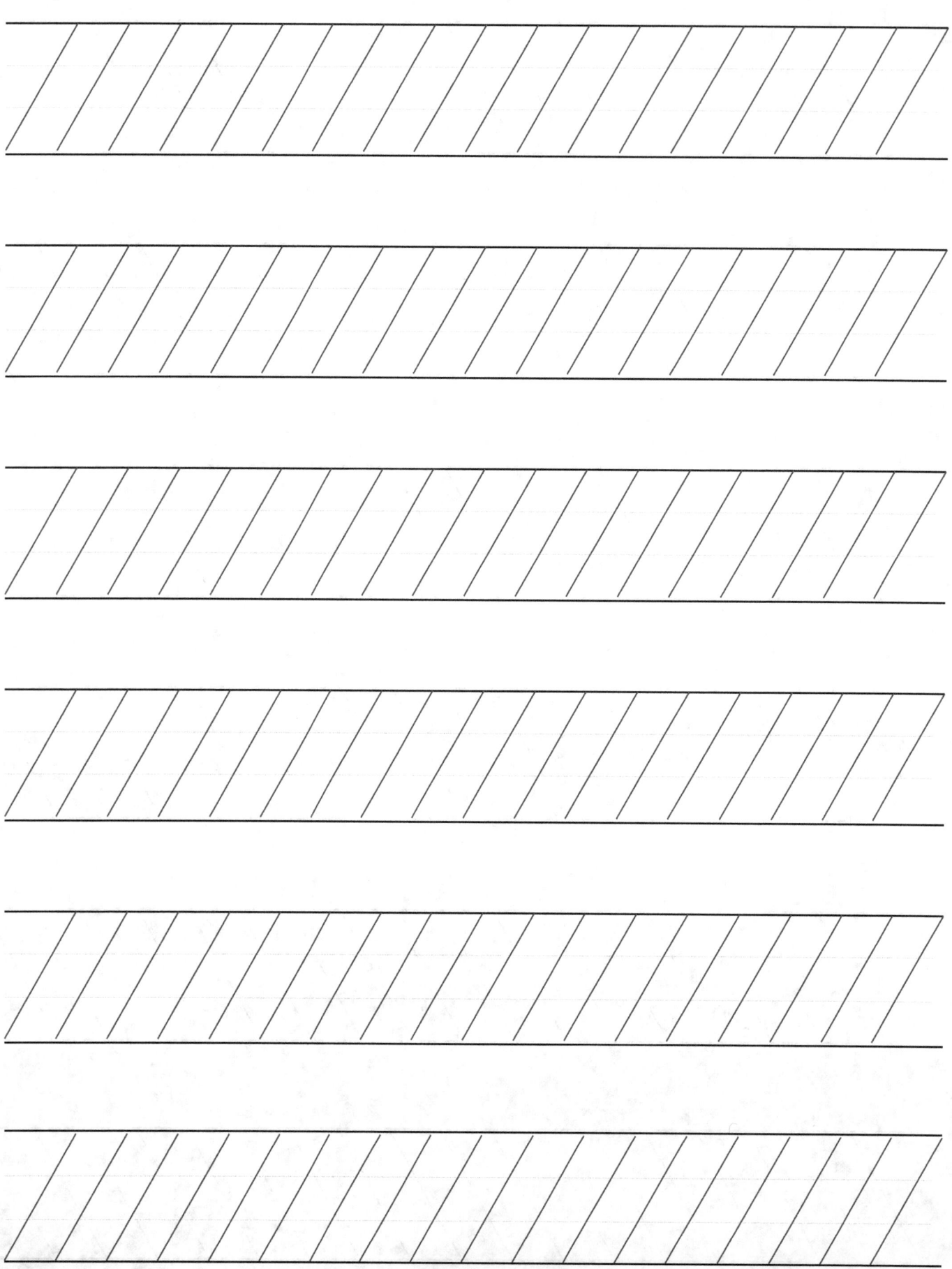

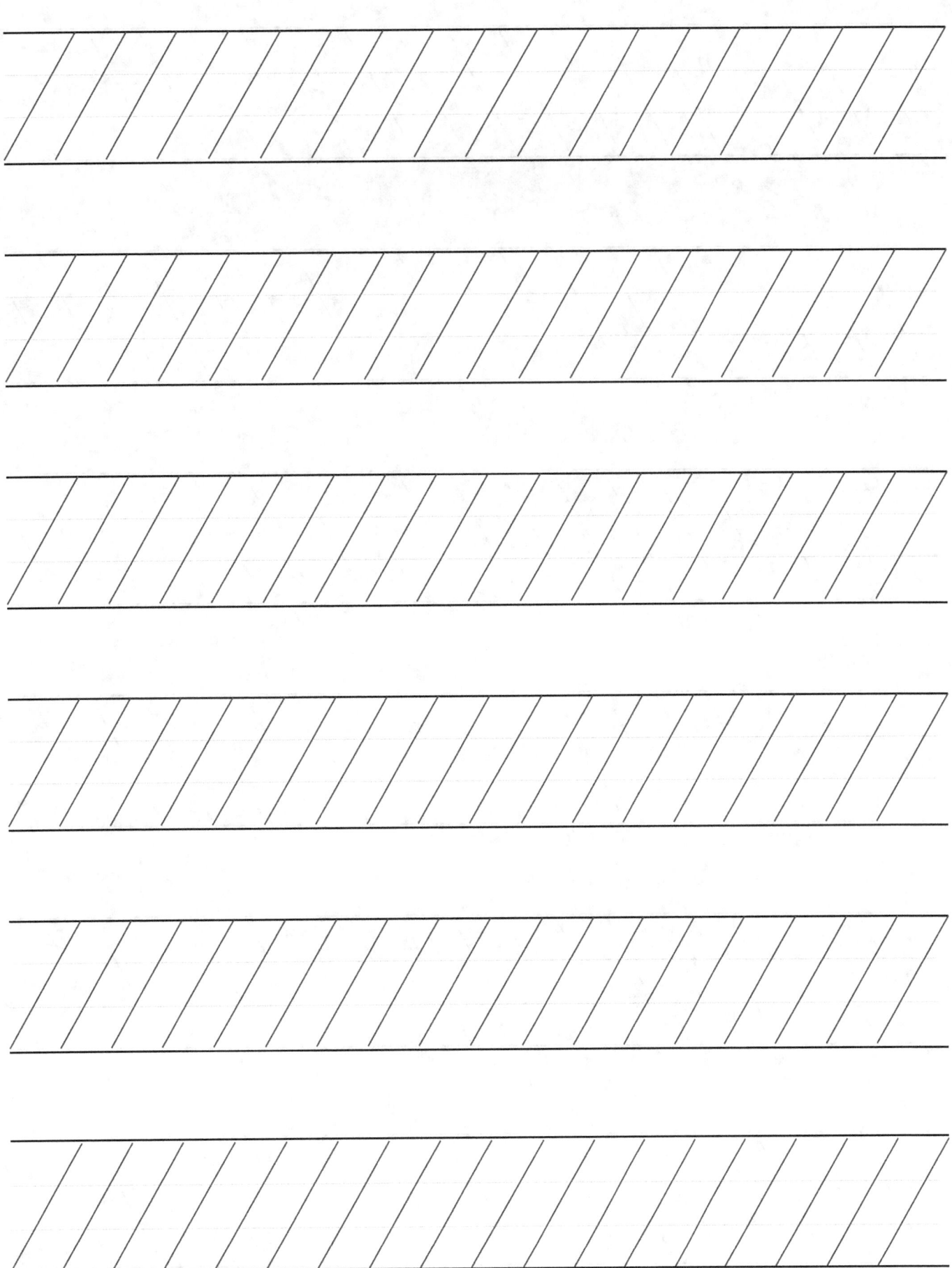

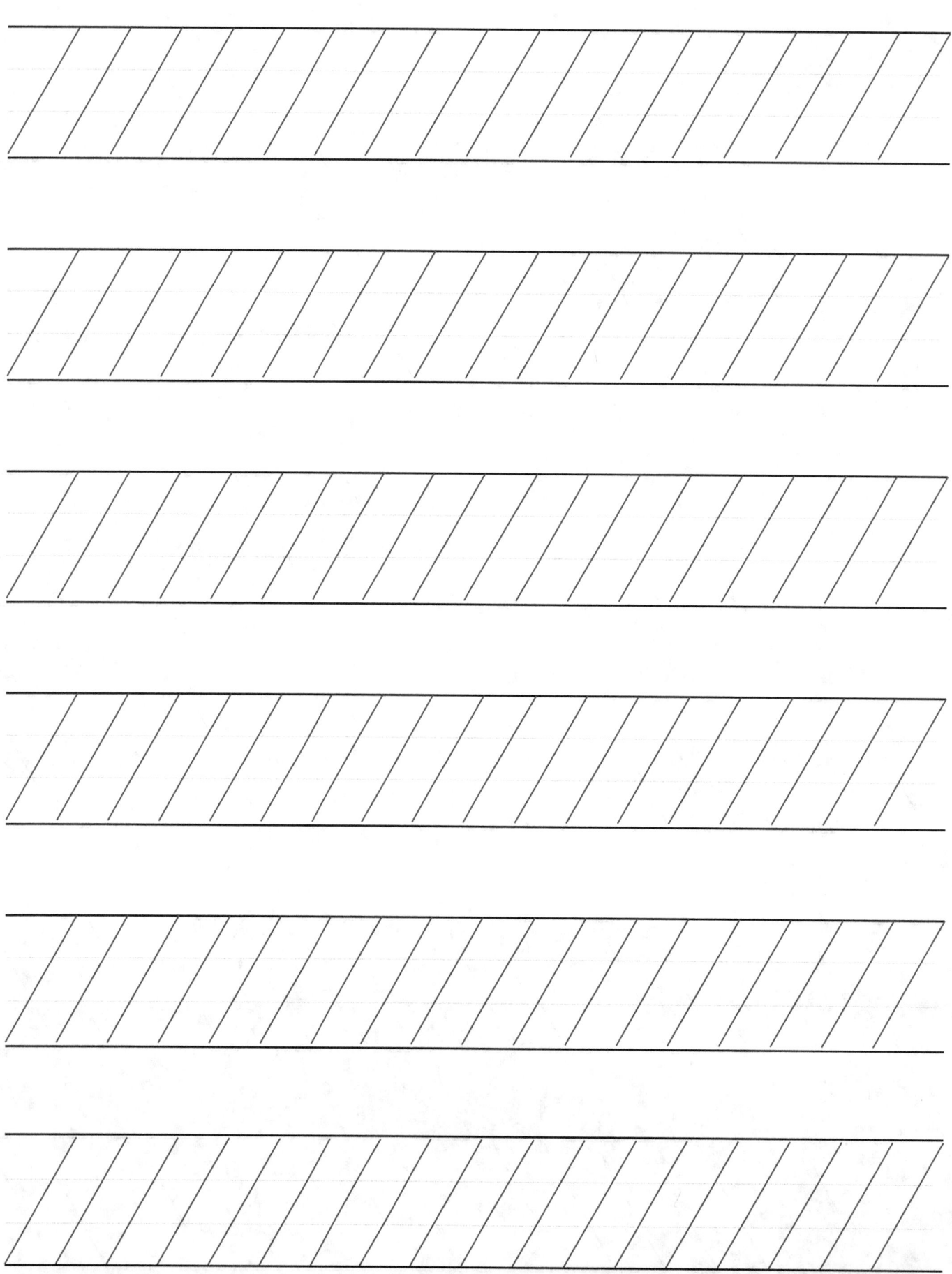

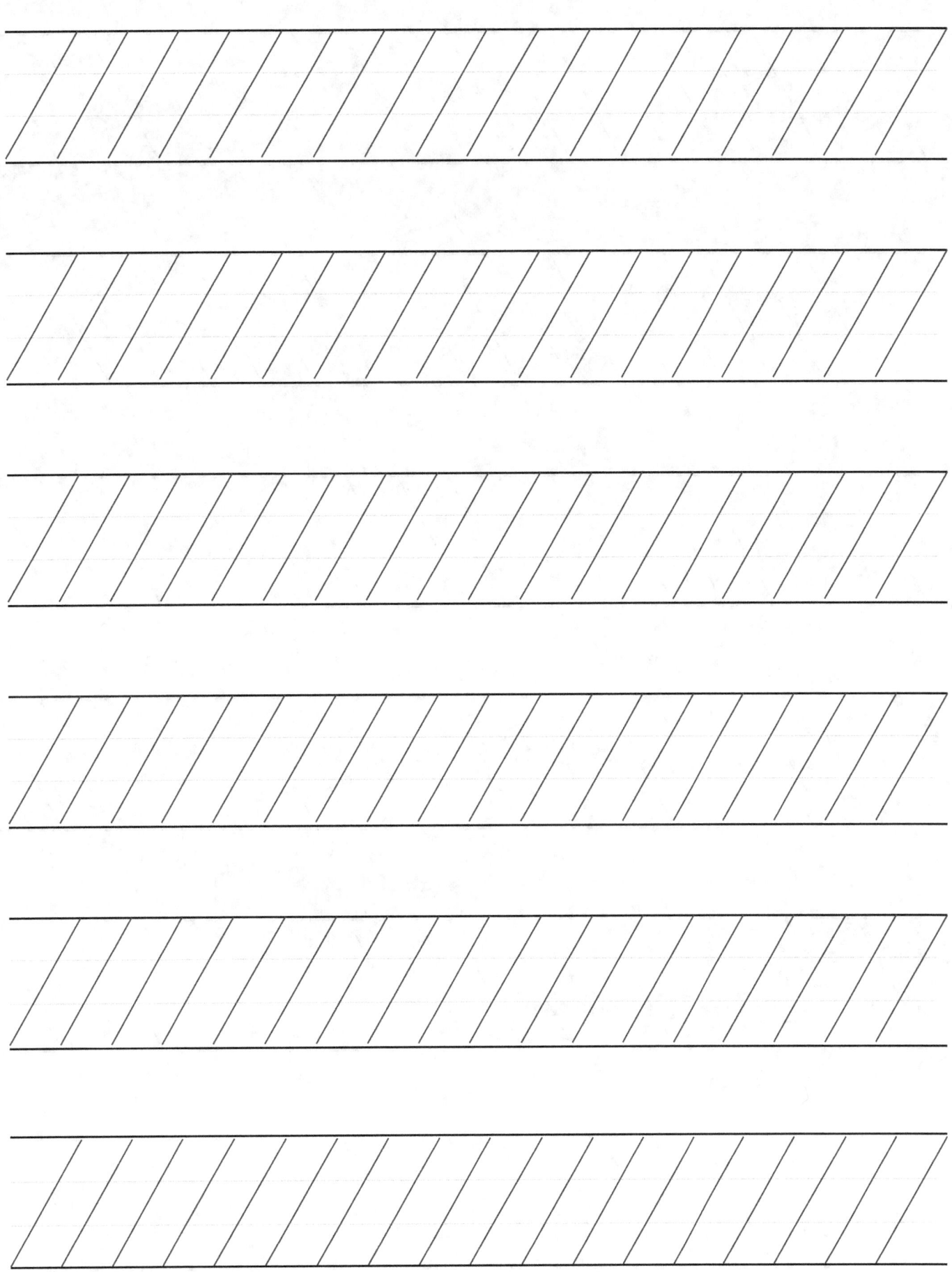

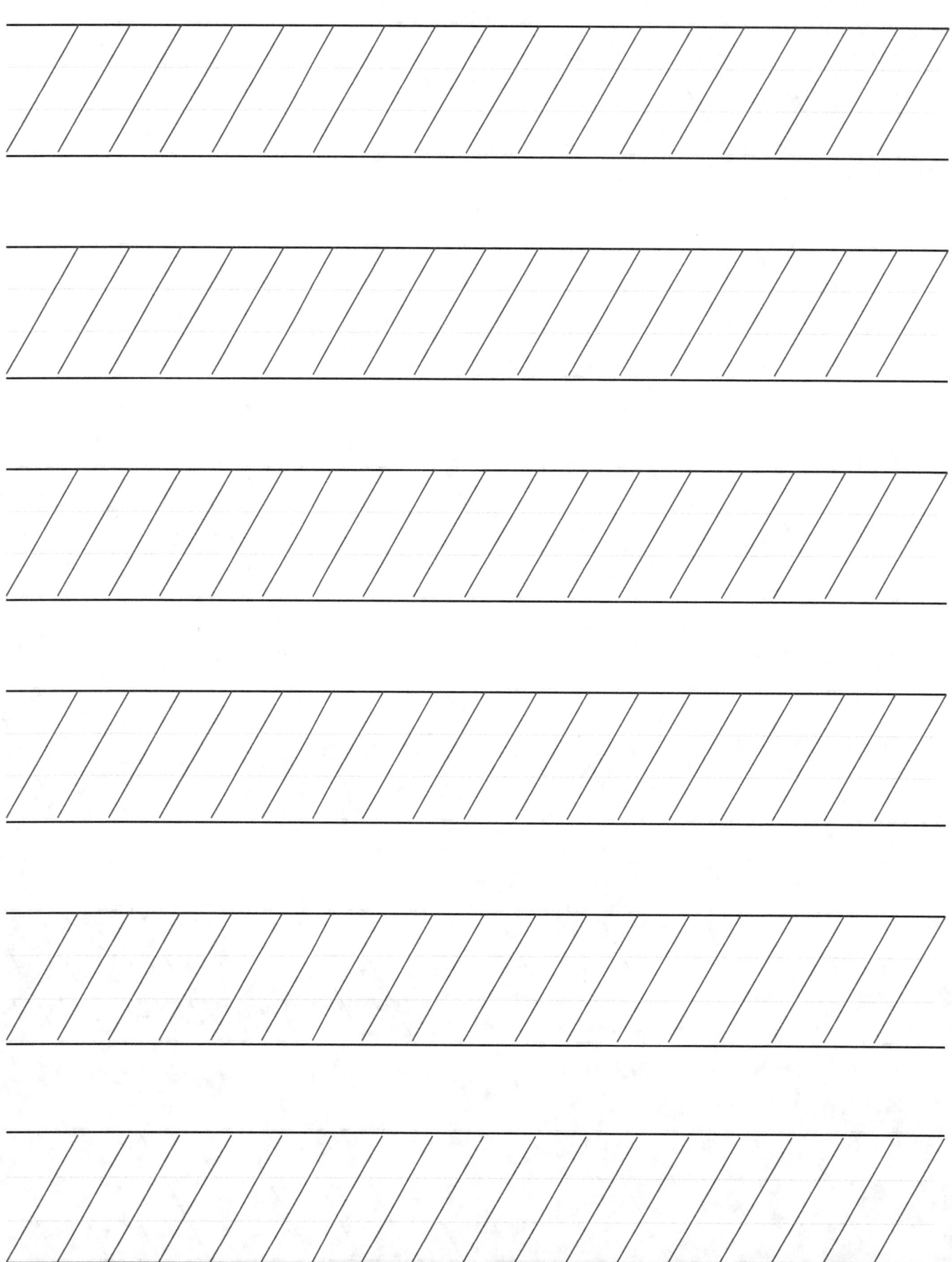

www.ingramcontent.com/pod-product-compliance
Lightning Source LLC
Chambersburg PA
CBHW060416220526
45465CB00008B/2904